John Simmons
THE MEASURE OF A MAN

BY
DENISE DOHERTY PAPPAS

Denise Doherty Pappas

John Simmons: The Measure of a Man
by Denise Doherty Pappas
Published by No Small Matters Press

Copyright ©2014 Denise Doherty Pappas

Epigraph: "Boston Firsts" by Lynda Morgenroth
Copyright © by Lynda Morgenroth
Reprinted by permission of Beacon Press, Boston

ISBN-13: 978-0692265208
Library of Congress Control Number:
2014913852
No Small Matters Press: Boston, MA

Cover photo courtesy of Simmons College Archives.
Images courtesy of Little Compton Historical Society
and Simmons College Archives.
Photograph of the author by Lora Brody.
Author website by Catherine Cairns.
Jacket design by Christa Johnson.
Graphics by Eileen Kenneally.

Photographs of paintings, images, and other materials from Simmons College Archives and Little Compton Historical Society archival collection courtesy of Sam Smiley.

Dedicated to Dean Pappas, M.D., my beloved husband,

a man's man, who has always measured up.

An institution is the lengthened shadow of a man.
~Ralph Waldo Emerson

With me, all deep feelings are silent ones.
~Henry Wadsworth Longfellow

But there is no one thing which men so rarely do, whatever the prov-ocation or inducement, as to bequeath patrimonial property away from their own blood. They may love other individuals far better than their relatives; they may even cherish dislike, or positive hatred to the latter; but yet, in view of death, the strong prejudice of propin-quity revives, and impels the testator to send down his estate in the line marked out by custom so immemorial that it looks like nature.
~from *The House of Seven Gables*, Nathaniel Hawthorne

One man or woman's inventiveness, insight and derring-do are at work in multiple *milieux*. Such is the case of John Simmons (1796-1870). His diverse accomplishments now seem logical, even or-dained. But during his lifetime, it would have seemed unlikely that a dour merchant of Pilgrim origin would become a feminist. Simmons exemplifies the potential of a man attuned to his time, or sufficiently ahead of it to self-propel, prosper and contribute to society, including after death.
~from *Boston Firsts: 40 Feats of Innovation and Invention that Happened First in Boston and Helped Make America Great*, Lynda Morgenroth

TABLE OF CONTENTS

FOREWORD

As the eighth president of Simmons College, I remind myself everyday of my obligation to steward the incredible investment John Simmons made with his worldly goods. His commitment to women's economic well being, so forward thinking in his time, is a remarkable inspiration as I consider the financial and strategic issues facing Simmons College today. And, his life and work provide compelling lessons for sustaining the mission, articulating the continued validity of women's education, and uncovering new growth opportunities for our programs. Continuously seeking to understand the experience and motivations of our founder has enriched my tenure as president, but my appetite for information has been somewhat stymied by the dearth of available history. With the publication of this book, Denise Doherty Pappas has made a dramatic advance in our understanding of this important man. Her work gives rich insights into a mind dedicated to commercial success, improved life circumstances, and using those personal gains to aid others in their own prosperity—doing good by doing well.

President Helen Drinan
Simmons College
October 2014

INTRODUCTION:
A WOMAN'S WORK IS NEVER DONE

Let all men know thee, but no man know thee thoroughly.
~Benjamin Franklin

We all have our heroes. When I was a student at Simmons College, my mother, Dot Bechan Doherty, was my ideal. The daughter of Czech immigrant parents, Mum was the original domestic goddess. She sewed all my childhood clothes, made our drapes, slipcovers, and bedspreads. She cooked divinely, was a bathing suit model, and was the first woman to sign a contract with the National Football League as office manager with the New England Patriots, headquartered in Foxboro, Massachusetts. Who wouldn't want to be like my mother?

For this reason, I selected a home economics class that included making a Vogue patterned dress. I had never even sewn on a button and felt awkwardly unprepared. Despite having a great instructor, I remained all thumbs. Yet this didn't worry my mother since she had higher aspirations for her daughter.

Wise to the ways of social acceptance, my mother insisted I have all the right outfits for college—meaning store bought. Freshman year I landed in a two-closet triple. My John Meyer of Norwich-inspired wardrobe hogged one and a half closets, leaving two roommates sharing the remaining half a closet space. Back home, my mother had forbidden me to wear blue jeans, but I couldn't abide by this rule. Borrowing my roommate's worn pants was my most rebellious act—and this was the late 1960s!

At that time, I had no idea that my mother and I were both acting out the centuries-old ritual of upward mobility in America. Clothes made not only the man, but the woman who wished to be noticed. The better the wardrobe, the better the life. Dressing for success was standard operating procedure.

What I didn't know then was the pivotal role my college's founder, John Simmons, had played in making this material world possible. I didn't know it was his fortune, based on a successful and lucrative manufacturing business producing ready-to-wear clothing decades before the sewing machine was invented, that had helped thousands of people rise in the world of work. I didn't know that a century before, John Simmons was rooting for me, a third-generation Irish-Czech girl, to get the best education for an independent livelihood. As a student at the college named in his honor, I had no knowledge of John's life story, or of our "ready-made democracy" linking increasing material and social progress with civic participation, and of its profound effects on my own life and times. Years of personal experience observing businessmen and philanthropists revealed tantalizing bits of John's biography, and through my research on the college's founder, I began to connect significant dots between our times and his.

While at Simmons, I took my education for granted. For me, attending a women's college was the best of both worlds. During the week, I focused on my studies. I dressed down and didn't worry about my social life off campus. I enjoyed the sisterhood I found at Simmons—women were respectful, helpful and simpatica. In class, my fellow students were cooperative, not cutthroat. Being at a same-sex college made for instant identification, a shorthand for like-minded souls. We listened to one another, we explored and discussed our emerging voices and visions, we supported and encouraged each other. For me, the bonus of Simmons was the chance to absorb the behaviors and values of an educated feminist majority. Post-class time was time enough for the opposite sex.

After Simmons I went to graduate school at Brown University, where my work habits changed. In Brown's co-ed classrooms, I found myself paying more attention to my appearance than to my schoolwork. Books took a back seat to being well dressed, and I focused less on my studies and more on my social life. Although feminism was on everyone's lips, there was still much to overcome. After four years at a same-sex school I found the dynamics of romance, including showing off in the clothes of the times (mini-skirts, hip-riding jeans and gauzy tops) compelling.

Graduate school was challenging but I missed the collegiality of same-sex classrooms. Even though the times were changing, and women were fighting for equality in all arenas, it often felt like men dominated the classroom. When Simmons established its School of Management exclusively for women, I knew immediately that it was the perfect graduate degree program for me. Simmons College's unique MBA program opened my eyes to both the gender diversity in business and the similar approaches women share with men in operations, management and behavior, and entrepreneurship. With a broader understanding of business and gender, I graduated—a contented alumna once more.

Two experiences later deepened my appreciation for this rare institution, and provided my great awakening. First, living in Saudi Arabia before and after the Gulf War made me a Simmons fan in full force. I taught third graders at an international school in Jeddah and my husband, Dr. Dean Pappas, taught pathology to Saudi doctors in a program through Tufts Medical School. Over two decades ago, we worked in a country where the rights of women were dictated by religious belief and social custom. In Saudi Arabia women were prohibited from driving. They could not leave the country without the express permission of a grandfather, father, uncle, brother, or husband. Having spent time in Middle East I returned to Boston with a stronger appreciation for my Simmons College education and for my life in a secular, democratic country.

But intrigued by my Saudi experiences, I studied Islamic and Middle Eastern History and had the good fortune to teach writing to diplomats and government officials at The Fletcher School at Tufts University. My students came from Qatar, Saudi Arabia, Abu Dhabi and the Republic of Armenia. Over and over I saw that educated women were the best proponents for peace and prosperity.

In 2008 I taught the most remarkable group, thirteen newly-trained female diplomats from Saudi Arabia at Tufts. The backgrounds of these graduates of Dar El Hekma, a private women's college in Jeddah, reminded me of the historical struggles and victories shared by early college graduates in America. Their stories illuminated how profoundly an all female environment fosters independence and the conviction that women are extraordinarily capable. In short, educational institutions founded in the face of gender discrimination provide more than an education—they produce strong, self-confident achievers. In my decades of teaching, I found these Saudi women to be among the most courageous, ambitious scholars I ever encountered. How like my Simmons foremothers!

A second awakening came to me in 1992, when my dear friend Betsy McCandless—a strong, intelligent, fun-loving and thoughtful classmate from the class of 1971, was murdered by her ex-husband. In that especially isolating pre-OJ Simpson trial era when domestic violence was considered a private matter, Betsy had run from her terrifying husband, gotten a divorce, and trained in self-defense. Before she was murdered, Betsy was writing her own textbook on overcoming domestic violence. She wanted to give other women specific advice on personal and legal recovery. She was extremely brave, but equally unlucky. Despite her careful precautions, Betsy's ex-husband, in a deranged rage, stalked and shot her to death in December of 1992.

Betsy's brother, Steve McCandless, was devastated. He had made every effort to protect his sister. In spite of his own pain, Steve made and continues to make substantial efforts to expose systemic ignorance of relationship violence. Steve has become an exceptional brother to many as a tireless advocate and sponsor of REACH Beyond Domestic Violence in Waltham, Massachusetts and Safe Horizon in New York City.

Shortly after her death, Betsy's classmates, under the leadership of visionary activist Ruth Ginsburg (Class of 1971), gathered at the college and proposed a teaching opportunity as a memorial reflecting Betsy's courage. With the wholehearted approval of then President Dan Cheever, Simmons began "Betsy's Friends." It is, to my knowledge, the first college peer counseling relationship violence prevention program in the country. Protecting students is key at Simmons—a long established priority of which the college is justifiably proud.

Both my Saudi experiences and my association with "Betsy's Friends" made me aware of good and bad fortune, vigilant to the evolving timeline of women's rights and restrictions—that universal tightrope both sexes traverse. As I counted the good guys who were, as we said in the 1960s, "part of the solution, not of the problem," John Simmons topped my list.

To learn more about this philanthropist, I met with Simmons College's archivist. Jason Wood introduced me to the core college biography of the founder. Written by Professor (Emeritus) Kenneth L. Mark in 1945, *Delayed By Fire* includes a chapter on John Simmons' life. This institutional history made me curious for a more expanded biography of the man to whom I owe so much.

As I researched and wrote about John Simmons, I piggy-backed on the writings of others to describe this modest Little Compton, Rhode Island native: a man of public success and private sorrow. I included the ideas and life stories of Simmons' influential contemporaries to flesh out John's life and times. Noted biographer Richard Holmes wrote: "Biography is the broken bridge into the past." How true! But Google's lauded search engine offered little concrete information about John Simmons—I found no direct diaries, journals or business records of a man I had come to admire. I dug deeper, but huge information gaps kept him elusive. Most biographers won't touch a subject lacking primary resources, but what I did find was tantalizing, and so I've spent the last few years tracking down connections to the life and times of John Simmons. Perhaps future researchers will find more primary sources; I would welcome a more extensive study of John Simmons.

Had social media been present during John's lifetime would he have availed himself of the ability to post and tweet? Benjamin Franklin, with his Twitter-like proverbs and aphorisms would no doubt have found tweeting the perfect forum for spreading his wisdom. But John Simmons was an intensely private man and information about John came through indirect channels and sources. Yearning for more data I would often intone: "Speak for yourself, John." In the end, as man of "deeds, not words" Simmons' actions speak for themselves.

As a grateful alumna I had a raging curiosity to discover what motivated John Simmons. I was inspired to examine the life of the man whose far-sighted college endowment deeply affected my life. So many people's lives have been enriched through his mission, so many have benefited from careers he set in motion long ago. How and when and why family, friends, leaders, losses, current events and constant crises turned John Simmons from a frugal entrepreneur into a generous supporter of women's education and careers are themes I explore in this book. I hope to encourage questions, interpretations and perhaps elicit memories in response to this quiet philanthropist's mission. The long, strong thread between John's life and ours today tugs at heartstrings and minds alike.

I have made every effort to present an accurate, well-researched biography. In lieu of footnotes, an extensive bibliography can be found at the back of the book. To address existing biographical gaps, I employed a wide-angle lens. In this book, I share much social history of John's times without evidence as to how he responded to his contemporary issues. This biography of John Simmons should not be considered the last word on this generous man, for I have not attempted a scholarly or academic work. My goal is to give readers an opportunity to get to know a man whose legacy grows by the day, and to that end, I have omitted footnotes in favor of a lean narrative. As Voltaire wrote, "The most useful books are those of which readers themselves compose half." As you read this book, I invite you to find the connections between your life and the personal and career history of a nineteenth century Yankee who gave purpose to his mixed blessings through the founding and endowment of Simmons College.

"Each age writes its own biography." Ralph Waldo Emerson espoused and understood this. As we approach the two-hundredth anniversary of John Simmons' career in Boston, the interdependency and equality of the sexes remains a work in progress. In *John Simmons: The Measure of a Man* I hope to acquaint the founder of Simmons College with his natural constituency—today's readers who know that while "a woman's work is never done" it is best accomplished with the cooperation and support of women and men like this radical tailor-entrepreneur. In this way, we will ALL measure up.

Denise Doherty Pappas
October 2014

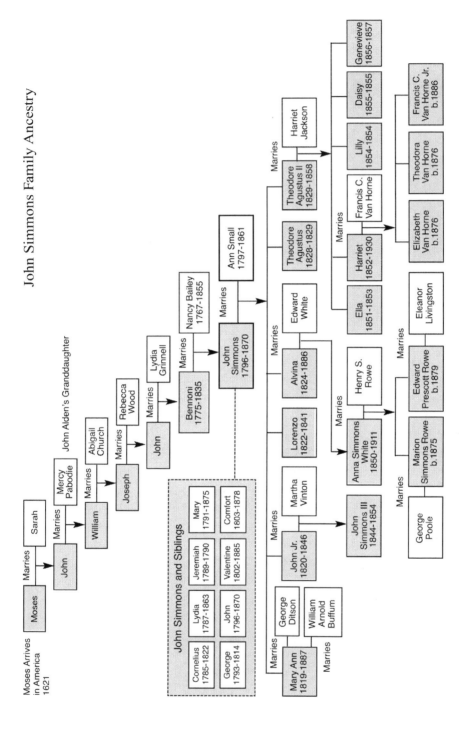

John Simmons Family Ancestry

Influential People in the Life of John Simmons

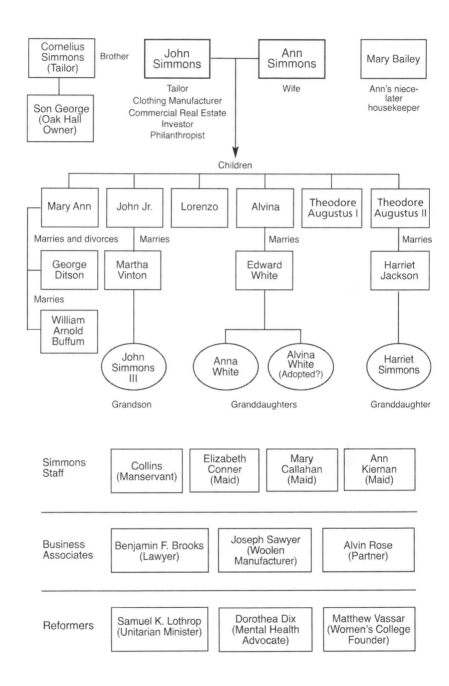

PROLOGUE: SIGN HERE

On June 1, 1867, John Simmons signed his will at the law office of Benjamin F. Brooks at 40 State Street in Boston. The contents of the will provided an endowment to Simmons College and ensured the education of thousands of women with unwavering emphasis on preparing for the world of work. Unfortunately, no documents have been found to describe what John Simmons was thinking that day. To illuminate a critical moment in the College's history, I based the following dramatization, which set in motion the founding of Simmons College, on what is known and on what I imagined. In doing so, I've taken creative license; however, the rest of the biography is based on factual information uncovered by extensive research.

"Collins, please return to the mansion." John Simmons, one of Boston's wealthiest men, gave this order as he stepped out of his well-maintained barouche.

"Today's business will take me a few hours," he said, checking his pocket watch to make sure he would be punctual for his one o'clock appointment. "Miss Mary Ann needs your services at home. Collect me here at five."

"Yes, sir," his Irish manservant replied in a thick brogue, having helped his carefully groomed seventy-year-old employer onto the city sidewalk at 40 State Street in Boston. The afternoon of June first 1867 was a temperate day, perfect for the long-planned work ahead.

In his signature long black coat with high collar and black cravat, John Simmons stood tall and slim, despite his age and chronic disease. He looked up at the lawyer's office he was about to enter.

"Benjamin F. Brooks," he said to himself, recalling the national hero Benjamin Franklin. "May my Benjamin be as wise as Mr. Franklin," John mused, remembering the progressive thinker for whom many a young man had been named.

John was confident he had chosen the right advisor for today's mission. Although a generation younger than John, Benjamin F. Brooks, the legal counsel for Jordan Marsh, a leading Washington Street department store, was later described as "a man needed every hour by merchant princes and business magnates" having "the success of character rather than intellect" and a "capacity for business rather than finished culture." Like his client John Simmons, Brooks was described as "free from all show, pretention and display."

That day in Boston, the Yankee magnate John had his mind on transformative action. During his carriage ride, John noticed an exhausted-looking young woman walking on the sidewalk with a large load of shirts under one arm, her other arm dragging a daughter beside her. Memories of women in reduced circumstances flooded his mind. From the war widows of 1812 to post-Civil War sole providers, visions of hard-working women tugged at his conscience. How many unskilled women had he turned away because they lacked appropriate training? How many souls were at the mercy of this capitalist metropolis? He thought, "Such lost potential!"—and it was this potential John sought to encourage and support through legal means. As he knocked at his lawyer's door, John sighed.

After four hours of detailed decision-making, fifty-one-year-old Benjamin Brooks paused and asked his client, "Are you quite certain you want to do this? Is this absolutely your intention?" Brooks rose from his mahogany chair, walked to the opposite side of his desk, and put his hand on his longtime friend's shoulder.

"Fairness is what I am after," John replied, his right hand grasping his fountain pen.

"As you wish," Brooks answered, and he excused himself to collect the legally required three witnesses.

This interlude gave John Simmons time to recall the people who had enriched his life, including his tireless father and calm-tempered, vivacious mother. John smiled, thinking of his beloved and beautiful wife Ann who had given him four sons. His grandson John III had been named in his honor. With these loved ones, John had shared fortune and misfortune, happiness and heartache.

He had been blessed with his two daughters, Mary Ann and Alvina, who had stepped in at their mother's passing. Six years a widower, John still enjoyed Sunday morning breakfasts with granddaughters Anna and Harriet.

With Brooks' assistance, the day's carefully conceived legal decisions had taken the form of a formal testament regarding John's estate, his plan for the coming years. "Thy will be done," Simmons whispered, mingling his will with that of the Lord's, as Brooks returned to the room with three office conscripts. Witnesses Horatio G. Parker, Henry Lunt and Fritz H. Rice were enlisted to bear witness to John's will.

"Do you have any second thoughts, any additions, or corrections?" Brooks asked. "Perhaps something you'd like to say?"

Sitting upright, John answered, "Hand me that document." The benefactor valued action over public proclamations. "Deeds, not words," John asserted, quoting Benjamin Franklin. "Give me the will. I am ready to sign."

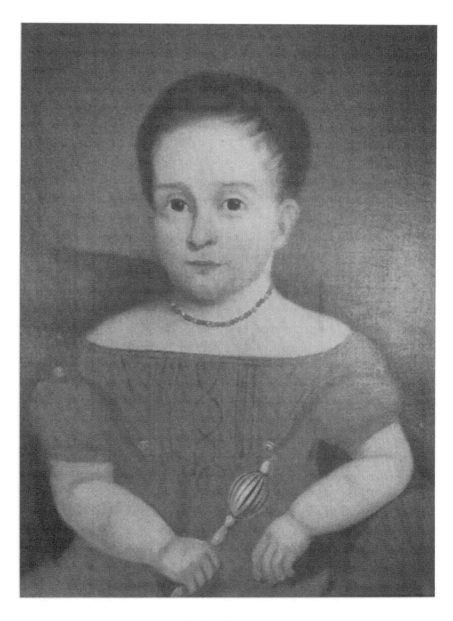

John Simmons

This oil painting from Little Compton Historical Society depicts a well-loved toddler. The outfit and pose foreshadow the wealthy gentleman John would become.

Nancy Bailey Simmons

Nancy Bailey Simmons (1767-1855), John's lovely mother, raised eight children.
A lifelong resident of Little Compton, Rhode Island, she lived to be
eighty-eight-years old.
Photo courtesy of Little Compton Historical Society.

The Simmons Family Home in Little Compton, RI, circa 1957.

Photo courtesy of Simmons College Archives.

CHAPTER ONE: FIRST FORTUNE

A good example is the best sermon.
    ~Benjamin Franklin

Founding Father

Most happy stories end with a fortune. This biography begins with one.

On November 9, 1621, Moses Symonson stepped off the ship in Plymouth Harbor. After three months of hard crossing on the Atlantic Ocean, solid ground was welcome relief. This Moses hadn't parted the waters, but he had traveled upon them from Leyden, Holland. His ship followed the *Mayflower*'s landing in Plymouth the year before. Moses, a young English pilgrim, was part of the second expedition to reach Massachusetts Bay. His ship was called *Fortune*, a sign of what each passenger hoped would come. A fellow shipmate among the thirty-five persons aboard the fifty-five ton ship included Phillip De La Noye of Leyden, who would later head the family of Franklin Delano Roosevelt.

Land acquisition was Moses' forte. Within two years he was assigned an acre tract of land in Plymouth. A 1627 division land grant describes him as an "unmarried man" who joined a consortium to lease four black heifers, a key commodity in the colony's fledgling years. By 1633 he had changed his name to Moses Simmons, and by 1638 he received a land grant of forty acres. Moses lived in Duxbury with his wife Sarah and continued to acquire property. In 1645 he received another land grant in Bridgewater, and by 1652, with a group of investors, he purchased twenty-four square miles of land with a three-mile waterfront from the Native Americans. In 1662 Moses bought land in Middleboro, Dartmouth, and New Bedford.

A fire destroyed town records prior to 1666, so Moses' date of birth and marriage are unknown. He and Sarah had seven children, presumably born between 1635 and 1650. The Simmons family founder died in Duxbury in 1689. In his will, every last shilling is accounted for, including the two pounds and ten shillings Moses gave to his daughter Sarah, claiming her husband "James Nash has 2 pounds and 5 shillings in his hands already." Moses' flair for real estate and a habit of financial accountability would be passed down to his descendants.

Enter the Aldens

In 1669, Moses' third child, John, married Mercy Pabodie, the granddaughter of John and Priscilla Alden. With their union, the Simmons family expanded to include some historically renowned seventeenth century ancestors. Priscilla Mullins and John Alden (later immortalized by poet Henry Wadsworth Longfellow in "The Courtship of Myles Standish") were America's "first couple."

Both lived in Plymouth in the early days of the colony; both had been passengers on the *Mayflower*. John Alden was a handsome barrel maker, and Priscilla a beautiful single woman residing with her father, William Mullins.

It's a well-known story. Captain Myles Standish, the leader of the Massachusetts Bay Colony, had lost his wife Rose to illness in January of 1621. Shortly thereafter, widower Standish sought a new wife. He sent his subordinate, John Alden, as a go-between to ask Priscilla's father for permission to marry his daughter.

According to the legend, William Mullins told John Alden the choice was Priscilla's to make. He summoned his daughter, who listened politely to John Alden's request to be Myles Standish's bride.

Then Priscilla looked directly into John's eyes and replied: "Speak for yourself, John."

Alden blushed and quickly departed. But he returned a second time and asked Priscilla, "Will you marry me instead?" Within a few months, the two were wed. Their union added a touch of romance to the Simmons family's Pilgrim ancestors, who otherwise would have been remembered as dour survivors of a harsh environment.

Little Compton, Rhode Island

In 1684, Moses' son, John Simmons, and his wife Mercy Pabodie Simmons moved to Little Compton, in what is now Rhode Island, but was then part of Massachusetts. (Rhode Island was officially founded in 1741.) Little Compton's seacoast peninsula of twenty-three square miles was seventy miles south of Boston. There, in a beautiful coastal village filled with marshes and ponds across the water from Newport, generations of Simmons family members followed the example set forth by their ancestors—hard work and thrift were solid family values. Little Compton neighbors described the family as fair-minded farmers and shipbuilders.

Bennoni and Nancy Simmons

Six generations after Moses, Bennoni Simmons, future father of John Simmons, was born in Portsmouth, Rhode Island on August 4, 1755. The third of seven children, his unusual name was one given by Puritan parents based on a biblical reference from Genesis 35:18 meaning "son of my sorrow." Bennoni's name would prove aptly chosen. By age seventeen, he was working as an apprentice to a shipbuilder in Providence, Rhode Island. John Brown, the well-known merchant whose family operated a shipyard at Fox Point, led an attack on the British customs schooner *Gaspee* in 1772. Bennoni took part in the raid. Years later, in a Revolutionary War widow's pension petition, Bennoni's wife would claim that her husband had dressed in Native American garb and helped in the burning of the *Gaspee*, an action that pre-dated the similarly subversive Boston Tea Party. Although it tried, the British government could not produce enough evidence to prosecute the *Gaspee* raiders. Bennoni then moved to Glastonbury, Connecticut for more shipbuilding work, but he soon returned to Rhode Island.

At age twenty, upon hearing about the Battles of Lexington and Concord, Bennoni immediately enlisted in the colonial army and fought in the Battle of Bunker Hill. As a soldier he helped fortify Dorchester Heights. He re-enlisted as a sergeant and served as Master Gunner on the war ship *Trumbull* on Lake Champlain, for which he was paid thirteen dollars a month. There, on October 11, 1776, in a battle with the British, Bennoni's left arm was blown off by an English cannonball. Nonetheless, he remained in military service from 1775 to 1786. He was recognized for his patriotism and courage during his lifetime.

After the war he returned home. It was reported that Bennoni, despite his handicap, could hew more timber with one arm than ordinary ship carpenters could with two. In nearby Little Compton, Bennoni met and wooed a young woman named Nancy Bailey whose father, Cornelius, had died when she was five years old.

Nancy was seventeen and Bennoni twenty-nine when they married on December 19, 1784. According to Nancy's diarist neighbor, Sarah Soule Wilbour, when Nancy's friends objected to her "marrying a poor man with but one arm she replied 'I had rather be hugged by that ONE ARM than all the rest of the arms in the world.'" Wilbour described Nancy as a "bright, cheerful energetic woman....Resolutely, she took upon her the curious responsibility and labors which lay before her and brought up her seven children in habits of industry and self-reliance which were invaluable to them when they left the little cottage near Seacconet Point to make their way in the wide world." Nancy and Bennoni had eight children (one died in infancy)—the babies were often spaced two years apart. Bennoni built the house they lived in with his neighbors' help. Community cooperation and family connectivity were cornerstones of the four-room house where this nine-person working class family lived. In 1819, Bennoni was appointed as a town officer in Little Compton, and the 1820 census showed him working in agriculture with his youngest son, Valentine.

John Simmons Arrives

Nancy and Bennoni's sixth child, John Simmons, born on October 30, 1796, would go on to make history. Growing up in a modest house in a rural community, John enjoyed hunting in the nearby woods and fishing off Sakonnet's piers. His favorite food was said to be jonnycakes, cornmeal pancakes made, in his case, with flour ground at his relative's mill. This Rhode Island recipe for johnnycakes originated with the Algonquin Indians and was a Sunday breakfast treat.

In colonial fashion, John studied in a one-room schoolhouse called Peaked Top School. Two books, *The Bay Psalm Book* and the *New England Primer*, instructed John in what his elders believed every good Congregational boy should know. Deep learning and spiritual preparation toward early death was a necessary catechism. In the *Primer*, the letter 'T' depicts a farmer with his scythe: "Time cuts down all/Both great and small." 'Y' shows a skeleton chasing a boy: "Youth forward slips/Death soonest nips." In the harsh environment of the early 1800s, this severe training may have prepared

14

eighteen-year-old John for the wrenching news that his twenty-one-year-old brother George had been lost at sea in 1814.

The Treaty of Ghent, which ended the War of 1812 against the British, was signed in December of 1814. Victorious, Americans had proved themselves strong and capable of self-defense and self-rule. This "Era of Good Feelings" was so labeled by *The Columbian Centinel* in Boston on July 12, 1817, the same year the New York Stock Exchange opened. Optimism and self-sufficiency character-ized the period. Wartime values like thrift and delayed gratification were giving way to post-war pent up demand for goods. During the war, the British blockade had prevented textiles from reaching America, and Americans had been forced to make their own clothes with their own material. In peacetime, however, much of the country was changing from a farming economy to an early industrial nation. Soon textiles would be domestically manufactured and ready-to-wear clothing would make its debut.

John's Vocation

Until 1814, John had lived a parochial life in a farming and fishing community. He knew all his neighbors. As a child, his job had been to fetch the butter from his family's well where it was stored to keep it cold. John was trained to fish and hunt to be self-sufficient. He had been raised in a family of craftsmen, ship and homebuilders skilled in their trades. By 1814, John no doubt knew by heart his father's stories about his Revolutionary War experiences in Boston. As would have been the case with most people of those times, John also knew that wealthy city people dressed elegantly and used silver, not pewter, at mealtimes.

Given his nature, it is likely that John read his local newspapers about the expanding opportunities in Boston. For the first time ever, in 1813, a Boston paper used the expression "clothing store." Because all clothes at that time were made at home or by tailors, a shop devoted exclusively to what is known today as "off the rack" clothing was a novelty. John's eldest brother, Cornelius, was already an established tailor in Boston with a shop at 15 Ann Street (now North Street) near Dock Square. Many of his customers were sailors who sought ready-made outfits for sea journeys. An increased demand for clothes was a sign of the changes to come, and this stirred John's entrepreneurial bent. The son of the countryside decided to join his brother Cornelius as his apprentice in the capital of the Bay State.

Once again, neighbor Sarah Soule Wilbour, eight years his junior, recorded her impression of John Simmons, this time as he left Little Compton for Boston: John was "dressed in a green baize jacket, with a small bundle in his hands and $5 in his pocket." The eighteen-year-old John would learn the tailoring trade from his twenty-nine-year-old brother. On the stagecoach heading to Boston, John must have been filled with excitement and trepidation. What adventures would soon be his?

John Simmons

*John's good looks may well have helped him in his career selling
ready-to-wear clothing.
Photo courtesy of Simmons College Archives.*

John Simmons

Perhaps Ann Small wore this miniature portrait of her young fiancé.

Photo courtesy of Simmons College Archives.

CHAPTER TWO: OPPORTUNITY KNOCKS

To succeed, jump as quickly at opportunities as you do at conclusions.
> ~Benjamin Franklin

The Road to Boston

John's ride from Little Compton to Boston in a ten-passenger stagecoach cost the equivalent of two days' worth of a skilled journeyman's wages. The carriage moved with considerable speed for the times—ten miles per hour, and the road itself was little better than a well-traveled dirt path in many parts. The jostling caused by ruts and dips in the road often sent passengers sailing sideways or up toward the ceiling. John's bumpy journey followed the northbound route, which may have passed by Slater's Mill, a company town started by an English immigrant.

Slater's Mill

Samuel Slater was well known for producing the first machines that spun cotton yarn using water power from the Blackstone River, a forty-eight mile long hard-working waterway filled with salmon and lamprey. Waterwheels dated back to Greek and Roman times, and using the force of rivers, water mills provided a steady supply of power in colonial times for the grinding of corn and other foodstuffs—and eventually other industries run by local entrepreneurs saw the possibilities of water powered mills. Financed by Moses Brown of Providence, Samuel Slater's mill had been operating for twenty years by John's day. It not only employed new technology but was famous for its management organization as well. Later called "The Rhode Island System," Slater's factory employed families with children in his advanced mills. These workers lived in company housing and shopped in company stores, which simply attached their wages, giving the owner a savings on cash outlays. Workers attended company schools and went to company churches—no need to venture far.

By the time of John Simmons' journey to Boston, the mill was the largest and most modern industrial building in America. Working conditions, however, were unhealthy. Too cold in winter, too hot in summer, the mill was rife with respiratory pathogens. Nonetheless, workers gladly moved from farm to factory for steady work and sometimes, higher wages.

As a tailor's apprentice, John knew he would need to obtain quality cloth. Traditionally, fabrics were either produced at home or imported. Homespun chintzes and calico cost one dollar a yard, the equivalent of a skilled craftsman's daily wage and twice that of a farm laborer. Now cassimere (plain or twilled woolen cloth), denim and other cotton cloths were manufactured in factories in the Bay State. Based on decreased manufacturing costs, demand for cloth rose even as the price for cloth decreased. With the advent of lower factory production expenses, most people would soon be able to afford a change of clothing.

Eli Whitney

John was heading to Boston, the capital of a region that called itself a *Commonwealth*. Part of that common wealth included benefits accrued to the public by the creative inventions of men like Eli Whitney, inventor of the cotton gin. In 1793, the same year Slater was opening his mill, Yale graduate Eli Whitney, age twenty-eight, invented the machine that revolutionized cotton manufacturing. The word *gin*—short for engine—was the mechanical device that removed seeds from cotton, formerly a labor-intensive task. Whitney claimed his inspiration came from watching a cat try to pull a chicken through a wire fence, removing feathers as a result—perhaps an apocryphal story that illustrates the cotton gin process. Astonishingly, one cotton gin could yield fifty-five pounds of clean cotton daily. While this invention was revered as an industrial gift to Southern planters, its implementation demanded a greater supply of raw cotton, a crop dependent on slave labor to produce, which increased the slave market in the colonies. With slaves bearing the greatest burden, cotton goods became America's chief export between 1820 and 1860. Cotton-producing plantations expanded and with this growth came an intensified reliance on slave labor—a Gordian knot entangling all those involved in cotton production and cotton-based businesses. As the market for cotton increased, the demand for African-American slaves grew—solidifying the institution of slavery.

Paul Revere

Like John's father Bennoni, Paul Revere was also a Revolutionary War veteran. In 1788 Revere established an iron and brass foundry in the North End of Boston and a copper factory in Canton, twenty-five miles from Boston, not far from John's route from Little Compton. Aware of the ravages of use and the elements, Revere turned to copper manufacturing because copper was more rust-resistant than iron, and in 1802, Revere's factory supplied six-thousand square feet of copper sheeting for the construction of the original Massachusetts State House. Always a market responsive businessman, Revere became a charter member of the Massachusetts Mutual Fire Insurance Company, which he helped establish after a major fire destroyed much of Boston in April of 1787. Fires were a constant threat to businesses in the emerging industrial nation, and fire insurance provided a financial safeguard.

Interestingly enough, while John Simmons was heading to Boston, Revere was circulating a petition asking the government for aid for Boston artisans (like himself) in protecting Boston from the British during the War of 1812. Like Revere, John had entrepreneurial ideas. John, too, would soon search for new business opportunities.

Class Structure in Boston

The class structure of Boston society was well established by 1814. At the top were the ruling elites, later called Brahmins. Often Harvard graduates, mostly Episcopalian, these men were venture capitalists, factory and land owners, international traders, and ship owners. Next came the professional class of ministers, doctors and lawyers, often children of the Brahmin elite seeking significant life-improving or philanthropic work apart from their family firms. The merchant class followed the professional class in this social pyramid. This ambitious class of entrepreneurs was often Unitarian, not necessarily Harvard graduates. Below them were the farming class, and near the base of the pyramid were working class men and women performing service work. Finally, slaves were at the bottom of society in this fledgling nation. Together, free blacks and slaves represented about four percent of Boston's population. John's journey to the capital was more than a geographic relocation. It was his first step up on the social ladder.

John was a thrifty, discreet Yankee, the son of a skilled craftsman. In this stratified post-war world, social positions depended on family background, religion and education. Although of Puritan stock, in Boston, John would always be an immigrant from Rhode Island. He had not completed secondary education, let alone attended Harvard College. He was not an Episcopalian. Nonetheless, he, too, would profit from investments and the systems put in place by these early venture capitalists, whose efforts were revolutionizing the production of raw materials for John's chosen profession.

23

Textile Trade

In 1814, the same year John ventured to Boston, Francis Cabot Lowell (1775-1817), India Wharf's developer and rum distillery owner, established the Boston Manufacturing Company on the Charles River in Waltham, Massachusetts, eleven miles from Boston. Lowell's was the first textile mill in America wherein all operations for converting raw cotton into finished cloth were carried out in a single mill building. In a revolutionary managerial move, Lowell hired women fifteen to thirty-five years of age from farm families to become textile workers in what became known as "The Lowell System."

Lowell paid his mill "girls" lower wages than he paid his men, leading to greater company profits. To offset the lower wages, enticements for these new female recruits included the social safety of living in company boarding houses chaperoned by older women, as well as a small number of educational opportunities. Lowell's system was highly cost-effective and his mill provided some of the cloth inventory that tailors like John Simmons would need.

The same year John headed to Boston, Abbott Lawrence of Groton, Massachusetts worked as an apprentice for his older brother Amos. Together these siblings formed a business importing goods from Britain and China. Later, when the nation changed from a sea-oriented to land-based economy, they would establish their own textile mills (Atlantic Cotton Mills and Pacific Mills) in Lawrence, a town named in their honor.

Both John Simmons and Abbott Lawrence worked in a region recovering from the War of 1812. During the war the British had blockaded Boston harbors, and no cloth was imported. After the war the British dumped huge quantities of cloth and other materials on Boston, making competition tough for the newly established local mills. Yet Americans were ready and eager for social and economic change, and demand for clothing to meet the fashions and requirements of the times rose as the population shifted from rural to city life. Over thirty thousand people lived in Boston at that time, all needing new clothes for new occupations in a new era.

City Life

Dock Square, near Faneuil Hall, was John's final stop on his seventy-mile journey. His brother Cornelius had a tailor shop a short distance away at 15 Ann Street, near the waterfront. The Boston Harbor area catered to sailors and itinerants, even as new businesses like Cornelius' cropped up.

At night, grog shops selling watered-down rum were part of this urban landscape. With the wharfs nearby, rowdy seamen patronized these drinking establishments; they sometimes sang bawdy songs with lyrics like these.

> Corydon and Phylis told how
> Ten thousand times he kissed her
> While sporting on the green
> And as he fondly pressed her
> Her pretty leg was seen.

And something else
And something else
What I do know
But dare not tell.

But by daylight, sober sailors would come to Cornelius as customers. They needed new pantaloons before shipping out.

John Simmons

What impression was John trying to create by sporting this beard?

Photo courtesy of Simmons College Archives.

CHAPTER THREE: PRODUCTION COSTS

Early to bed and early to rise, makes a man healthy, wealthy and wise.
　　~Benjamin Franklin

The Tailor's Trade

The Simmons brothers succeeded in adapting to the needs of their new customers, whose preferred attire mirrored the new dressing habits of city dwellers in an emerging industrial society—very different clothing from what they'd worn in their past lives as farmers or countrymen. Previously, a person's social position and employment were limited by the class into which he'd been born, and an individual's place in the social pyramid all but dictated what a person might make of himself. But change was blowing in on all fronts. In John's childhood, dominated by land-based activity with just a hint of industrial breakthrough, citizens prized hand-made goods that reflected their maker's self-sufficiency. Restraint of wants was stressed both in church and the public square—covetousness was seen as wicked. In America's agrarian society, one set of work clothes and another for Sunday best were considered adequate.

Only elites had larger, more elaborate wardrobes, which were often made with imported British cloth and notions. Their clothes were expensive, custom made by male tailors, each of whom had his unique method of measuring his clients. All this was done behind closed doors, because touching another's body was considered an intimate act. Standardized body measurements would not be established until after the Civil War. Great care and attention were given to wealthy clientele who paid only when satisfied with the workmanship.

After 1814, however, changes in customer behavior drove the clothing market. By the time John arrived in the port city the British blockades had disappeared, and commercial activity began to grow once again. An expanding clientele of sailors who needed immediate clothing supplies made their way to Boston's tailors. Sturdy trousers held up by suspenders (or braces as they were then called) would serve sailors well as they voyaged to England, Africa and the Caribbean. Shirts had starched white high collars that gave the wearer an erect profile. Undergarments (or underdrawers) were not universally worn at this time, although sailors generally wore a knee-length shirt which afforded additional lower body protection.

Apprentices to tailors worked from six o'clock in the morning to seven o'clock at night six days a week. Tailor shops were cramped, often no larger than twenty square feet. Sewing at night with whale oil lamps was difficult and expensive, and candles were luxuries as well. Early nineteenth century court inventory records show poor families usually owned only two candlesticks, while the wealthy homes often had six. No wonder Benjamin Franklin advised: "Early to bed and early to rise, makes a man healthy, wealthy and wise." To marry quality with the new speed required to produce ready-to-wear inventory was the profession's challenge, and adequate lighting was but one issue.

Facing competition from other tailors on Ann Street, the ambitious Simmons brothers solicited new customers during post-war prosperity. Tailors like John hailed customers from off the street, asking them to examine the merchandise hung in front of their shops. John and Cornelius acted as both salesmen and manufacturers. They measured, cut and sewed all the pieces themselves, working day and night to meet the increased demand. They were so busy with their growing customer base that in the 1815 Boston Business Directory, Cornelius changed his profession from "tailor" to "slop shop owner"—"slop shop" then being the term for clothing store. A traditional tailor expected to make individual items one at a time, while a clothing store had already produced multiple garments closer to "one size fits all" for a customer's inspection. What the Simmons brothers forfeited in elite custom business, they made up for with volume sales.

Around Boston

In 1818, during the time of John's apprenticeship, the cornerstone of Massachusetts General Hospital was laid. The hospital was a charity initially funded by the wealthy, but served the entire commmunity in the Commonwealth. Across the Charles River, Charlestown Hospital (later named McLean after a merchant's generous donation) was an institution that treated six-hundred mentally ill patients. Boston prospered with myriad activities, including that of doctors and their attendants in the medical profession, clerks on their way to the state government and counting houses, lawyers heading to the courthouse, and all manner of nineteenth century men heading to stores, trading houses, importing businesses and banks. Potential customers all.

The virtue of work was sometimes offset by vice. Boston's taverns served many alcoholics, some of whom used drink to treat physical pain and still emotional distress before pharmaceuticals and psychotherapy. At a time when alcohol was cheap and readily available and pure water less so, Dr. John Collins Warren founded the Massachusetts Society for the Suppression of Intemperance in 1823, and he advised his fellow physicians to refrain from prescribing alcohol to patients. His argument was based on what many saw as the country's need for a sober and disciplined workforce. On July 22, 1825, Mayor Josiah Quincy arrested tavern rowdies in hopes of banishing "the nymphs of Ann Street" who languished a few doors down from John's business.

In 1818, after four years of apprenticeship, John set up his own business at 14 Ann Street. No record exists to explain John's sudden departure. Was this move pre-planned? Did John's business ideas conflict with his brother's? Was there an argument between the two? Or was there so much business that it was an amicable split? In the absence of evidence, *cherchez la femme*!

John and Ann

John's move to open his own business coincided with his marriage to twenty-one-year-old Ann Small of Provincetown, Massachusetts on October 29, 1818, the day before John's twenty-second birthday. Ann was a seventh-generation descendent of Edward Small, a 1637 immigrant from Biddeford, England, who had settled in Kittery, Maine. Edward's son Francis moved to Truro, Massachusetts on Cape Cod where Ann's parents, Daniel and Anna, lived. Ann was a strikingly handsome, fashionably dressed, brown-haired, brown-eyed woman. Since nearly all women of Ann's age were trained to sew, she would have brought sewing skills to her marriage. Tailors often married women with sewing skills who helped augment their husband's incomes.

Nothing is recorded about John and Ann's courtship or her role in John's business life. However, courtship in the 1800s included marriageable young women paying extended visits to relatives in faraway locations, and relatives often took on the role of matchmakers. John's mother's maiden name was Bailey, and Ann's niece was Mary Bailey (the daughter of Lemuel Bailey and Ann's sister Ruth). Packet ships regularly traveled from Boston Harbor over the Atlantic to the Cape, saving passengers the one-hundred and twenty-three mile land trip that separated Provincetown from Boston. Ann may have sailed on a packet ship to Boston to be with family and to find an eligible bachelor. To add to potential romance, courtship lyrics of popular songs (like these below) harmonized the happiness of marriage in a family oriented society.

O share my cottage, gentle maid
It only wants for thee
To give a sweetness to its shade
And happiness to me.

Few people remained unmarried in the days when the average person wed between the ages of nineteen and twenty-three. While rural couples favored springtime or Thanksgiving weddings, urbanites were not restricted by the harvest calendar. The bride did not customarily wear white in this era and the couple was usually married at a relative's home. Newlyweds were often treated to a shivaree—a fun-filled serenade relatives provided for the couple on their wedding night. "A compassionate marriage" was the presumed goal of nineteenth century unions that kept partners emotionally fulfilled and economically productive, according to historian Catherine Kelly.

Reverend Thomas Baldwin, a sixty-five-year-old Baptist minister, performed the marriage rites for the couple in Boston on October 29, 1818. Baldwin was a trustee at Brown University and an 1816 founding member of the Provident Institution for Savings in Boston. The bank's mission was to serve "the frugal poor"; the lending institution approved many loans to textile merchants because its leaders were local lenders sympathetic to the risks and rewards of customers like John Simmons in the area's new industry.

Honeymooners John and Ann resided at 48 Ann Street, a short walk to John's 14 Ann Street venture. At that time, the average marriage produced seven children. Firstborn Mary Ann came just

34

shy of John and Ann's first anniversary in 1819. The next year, a first son, John Jr., arrived, followed two years later by a second son, Lorenzo, in 1822. In 1824, a second daughter, Alvina was born. Four years after Alvina's birth, Theodore Augustus came along, but died at eleven months. Unfortunately, it was typical for one in six children to die in infancy in those days. Yet Ann and John had little time to grieve for Theodore. Six weeks after his death his namesake, Theodore Augustus II, arrived and completed the Simmons family. The 1820s were a busy decade for Ann Small Simmons, to say nothing of her spouse. A Boston tax report shows John paid taxes on eight-hundred dollars worth of personal property and eleven-hundred dollars worth of real estate on Ann Street in 1822.

Many Changes

That same year, four years after John established his tailor shop, thirty-seven-year-old Cornelius died of consumption, leaving behind a ten-year-old son, George. During his brother's brief life, radical changes had occurred in consumer behavior. Cornelius was three years old when George Washington was inaugurated in 1789. America's first president, a citizen rather than monarch, dressed in a suit of brown broadcloth worn with pride because the material was American made, woven in a Blackstone River mill. Social conditions had also changed by the time Cornelius died. An emerging middle class required a different wardrobe to reflect its improved status. New clothes could produce respect.

Dressing for Success

In the new economy, to be better dressed meant to raise one's standard of living. The self-made man was now to be admired, not scorned. Although some feared the social changes inherent in material progress, dressing became a central event in modern life. Acquiring more goods was now perceived positively, an indicator of improvement in both work ethic and status. Early on, John realized the benefits of new purchasing habits. With ready-to-wear clothing (a predecessor of off-the-rack clothing), even if a customer was too poor to employ a custom tailor, by purchasing a ready-made outfit, he could rise from shame to respectability. With a socially acceptable change of costume, one became presentable, that is, "suitable" in the evolving culture.

John was intimately familiar with the desires of ambitious newcomers like himself. Unlimited possibilities for white males replaced knowing and remaining in one's place. Observing the changing habits of social classes, and noting his customers' similar physical sizes, John became an early creator of ready-made suits. Ready-to-wear manufacturers used three standard measurements to craft ready-made shirts. This saved on labor compared with the sixteen markings needed to finish custom clothes. John produced ready-to-wear clothing a decade ahead of Brooks Brothers, a firm on Catherine Street in New York City. They followed the trend adopted earlier by John Simmons and produced ready-made outfits for California-bound mining speculators in 1849. Indeed, by the 1840s, John Simmons, father of five living children, had become one of the most successful clothing manufacturers in all of Boston.

How did he accomplish this? Here's how.

First, in 1826, he moved his store from Ann Street to 51 North Market Street, a location closer to the newly established Quincy Market, a prime business address. There he displayed his inventory in the glass windows of his larger establishment. Drawn to the window display, customers entered his shop where more items were on view. Once inside, customer service and fixed prices (a novelty at the time) made Simmons' store the place to shop. John profited from new sales techniques, an expanding middle class market, and economies of scale in manufacturing. As a wholesaler, he artfully balanced his textile suppliers, his workers and his customers. As a salesman, John capitalized on his customers' desire to dress correctly.

Suiting One's Self

In 1827, Ralph Waldo Emerson defined the era as "the age of the first person singular." The emerging economy had few institutional constraints and the market revolution (wherein technology made consumer goods less expensive to buy) fostered changing consumer behavior. In *Making the American Self,* historian Daniel Walker Howe describes new and abundant choices—new technologies provided cheaper books, a variety of newspapers, lower postal rates. Libraries and lyceums gave Americans the opportunity for freedom of expression through reading and scholarship. New church denominations provided an array of transformative beliefs and phi-losophies. Self-definition became a way of life in America.

By 1841, Noah Webster included sixty-seven new words be-ginning with "self" to his American Dictionary. Some physicians worried that overconsumption was "moral insanity" but because of the "seduction of the shop" merchandizing flourished in Boston and beyond. Customers now expected a variety of choices. As Boston's population had tripled between 1820 and 1840, Simmons had many "selves" to serve.

John's Employees

John had significant help from the labor pool of tailors and seamstresses he employed. Early in his life, John observed his moth-er making the most of her time in a farming community. Like most everyone in rural communities, Nancy Simmons was one step ahead as she prepared for the coming season. In his business, John replicat-ed her pattern. Traditionally, spring and fall were "off season" sew-ing times. But John kept his tailors and seamstresses busy year round making summer and winter goods in advance of their sale date. That way, when customers came to the shop they had a larger inventory to select from.

John's tailors (all male) were paid standard wages: two dol-lars a day for their work in the shop. In the same time period, female seamstresses received fifty cents for their day's labor.

A key element in John's financial success came from divid-ing clothing manufacturing into piece-work. Tailors cut the fabric with precise and rapid strokes. They were trained to maximize each piece of costly fabric, the businesses' biggest expense. It is possible John purchased cloth through a commission agent representing Francis Cabot Lowell's Boston Manufacturing Company in Waltham. These tailor-cut pieces were then assigned to seamstresses (often war widows from the War of 1812 or farm women working for extra funds during their "off season"). Two decades before the sewing machine was invented, women hand sewed the pieces together in their own homes, saving John Simmons the expense of more factory space, which added to his profit. Seamstresses would return to John with finished outfits. Per customary wage practices, they were paid only for the sewing work that passed a strict inspection.

In this way, John kept fixed costs down as much as possible and passed some of the savings on to his customers. Ready-made clothes sold for half as much as custom wear. John benefited from the continually lowered cost of local fabrics as American legislators slapped protective tariffs on British goods. Having mastered the art of negotiating with rough sailors in his brother's shop, John was able to use smooth but aggressive sales tactics with working clientele who sought to establish their status through their clothing. By establishing fixed prices for all his goods, John relieved buyers of time consuming haggling. Because his customers were buying ready-made products with fixed prices, servants were often sent to collect the clothing, sparing working customers' time and travel expense.

The young man who had journeyed from Rhode Island to Boston by stagecoach now made the most of advances in transportation. In 1825 the Erie Canal opened. Begun in 1817, this three-hundred and sixty-three mile long public works project facilitated regional trade between the Great Lakes and the Eastern seaboard. With this new distribution channel, Simmons' goods could be sent directly to upstate New York at a transportation rate reduced by ninety percent. In the 1840s, John used the newly built railroads, which traveled twice as fast as stagecoaches, in two ways: to receive just-in-time inventory from mills in Waltham and Lowell, and to send a Simmons sales force West and South to take clothing orders from more rural locations. Simmons may also have used packet ships that sailed regularly from New York to New Orleans.

Simmons' Reputation

John Simmons received rave reviews in the 1848 publication of *The Stranger's Guide to the City of Boston*, a pamphlet written for out of town buyers and visitors. His character was described in this guide as "most firm and favorable"; his clothing "speaks for itself." His rooms, in a new locale above Quincy Market, were "capacious and well arranged with a vast amount of stock in hand." Altogether, the guide reports customers see "tangible evidence of the popularity of this place." The review ends by telling potential buyers that "Mr. Simmons is one of the oldest dealers in the clothing trade now doing business in Boston. He employs none but the most skillful cutters, and the organization of his establishment, the fairness of his team, the fidelity with which his garments are made up speak volumes in his favor."

Buyers from clothing stores from other regions, as well as individual customers, shopped at John Simmons' retail and wholesale store as clothing manufacturing became one of America's largest national industries. The company Dun and Bradstreet began its life as a vetting service checking the credit-worthiness of wholesale buyers who were John Simmons' potential customers.

John's Nephew, George Simmons

The clothing business had few barriers to entry, and Simmons' competitors were many. In 1842 John's thirty-year-old nephew, George Washington Simmons, firstborn son of John's brother Cornelius, opened Simmons Wholesale and Retail Cheap and Fashionable Cloth and Clothing Establishment at 33-36 Ann Street, the same street where Cornelius and John began their careers. Just as his Uncle John prospered by his wholehearted adoption of ready-to-wear, George proved to be a marketing and advertising genius. An immensely creative merchandiser, George published and sold Charles Dickens' *Pickwick Papers* from Simmons and Company's New Library at his North Street location for five cents a copy. In the book, George artfully advertised his store and included a full-page ad for Dobbins' Electric Soap. If a customer turned in fifteen soap wrappers, the ad promised, the Dobbins soap company would send back "first class sheet music for the piano." Advertising revenue added to George's bottom line.

When his business prospered, George enlarged his shop, renaming it Oak Hall. A huge retail and wholesale clothing store, it was renowned for its beautiful architecture and for its owner's outrageous sales techniques. George became famous for standing on the roof of his tall store throwing down free clothes to attract customers below. He used balloons to advertise sales. Some balloons contained coupons redeemable for free clothes. He even published a pictorial magazine to entice a new market: juvenile males. Inside George's catalogue were verses like this:

> This is the splendid stock in trade
> Comprising rich clothing, all ready made,
> Of every fashion, rank and grade
> Sold by the clever who faithfully work
> In the famous 'Oak Hall' on North Street.

George also excelled in effective pricing. On September 27, 1849, *The Boston Daily Atlas* reported "A friend, who was newly dressed in the most fashionable style, told us recently, that by purchasing in Oak Hall, he saved ten dollars on the suit. Such facts are important." Clothing business historians such as Arnold J. Karr in *Two Centuries of American Men's Wear* continue to praise George's long admired industry leadership. "[George] Simmons was a master promoter, worthy of emulation…he is credited with a number of 'free' firsts as well: free deliveries, use of outside salesmen and a mail order department, believed to be the first in any store."

George's showplace was famously upscale with its stained glass windows and skylights, a huge rotunda, lights lit by twenty-four gas burners, and pillars of "the Corinthian order." In 1861, John Wannamaker copied the name Oak Hall in his Philadelphia store, trying to capitalize on George's strong reputation as a retail merchant. Like his Uncle John, George Simmons was considered a leading clothing retailer. In newspaper advertisements in the 1840s, George's most clever and creative store advertisements ran side by side with John's more factual fare.

George's obituary in 1882 credited the seventy-year-old businessman as being the first clothing manufacturer to take full advantage of newspaper advertisements. The December 18th *Boston Daily Advertiser* described his temperament thus: "He was watchful over everything that would tend to increase its prosperity. He knew all his employees and made a large contribution to save the Old South Church." He was characterized as "gentle and retiring in disposition and manner." He brought "untiring zeal, energy and perseverance to every enterprise he undertook. Just and kind, beloved by those in his employ."

Uncle and nephew were cut from the same cloth. John led the industry in adopting and expanding the ready-to-wear market, while George reigned as an early advertising genius. Both men appear to have been prudent businessmen. Following the Depression of 1837, in March of 1838 John and George petitioned the Boston City Council asking the government to postpone a proposed water retrieval project for Boston. Their petition follows.

> We feel we ought to deny ourselves this luxury in common with many others until our means will afford their use; that we are now in a diseased condition, and unable to bear an additional burden; but restore us to health and prosperity, and we will again

jog on with such a burden as you may please to load us, in reason.

On a family note, when George's eleven-month-old son Frank died of whooping cough in 1844, he was buried in John Simmons' plot at Mount Auburn Cemetery.

No other evidence has been found to shed light on either the professional or the personal relationship between John and his nephew George. Both were silent to the end.

Ann Small Simmons

As the wife of a prosperous clothing manufacturer, no doubt Ann Small Simmons (1797-1861) paid close attention to detail in her wardrobe for her mid-life portrait.

Photo courtesy of Simmons College Archives.

The Simmons Mansion

Directly across from the Boston Common, 133 Tremont Street was a most fashionable address when the Simmons Family built their five-story mansion next to the Cathedral Church of St. Paul in 1841.

Photo courtesy of Simmons College Archives

46

CHAPTER FOUR: TIMES AND TREASURES

A penny saved is a penny earned.
      ~Benjamin Franklin

Moving On

In 1829, the year of Theodore II's birth, the Simmons family moved out of the North End to 17 Staniford Street, located in the more fashionable West End. As Boston's population grew, the Simmons clan desired more space for themselves. By 1840 Ann Small Simmons was forty-three-years old, the mother of five surviving children. Mary Ann was twenty-one, John Jr. twenty, Lorenzo eighteen, Alvina sixteen and Theodore eleven. John had successfully expanded his tailoring business into a large scale manufacturing operation, which handled the fabrication, sales and delivery of men's ready-to-wear to his customers. So once again, the family was on the move. John had located a more prestigious address that reflected his financial prosperity.

Final Resting Spots

The route between Staniford Street and the new family home on Tremont Street passed by numerous Boston landmarks such as the King's Chapel Burial Ground. John's father, Bennoni, had died five years before and was buried in Little Compton. His father's death at almost eighty made John aware of his own mortality. Planning for the future, in 1837 John purchased a burial plot for himself and his family at the newly opened Mount Auburn Cemetery across the Charles River in Cambridge. Although John and his wife and family were thriving at this time, frequent infant deaths and a multitude of incurable diseases marked the era—and John Simmons was well aware of the Psalter's warning: Death could appear at any time.

John's purchase of a plot at Mount Auburn reflected his generation's changing attitudes toward death and remembrance. Unlike the simple resting place in the graveyard of Little Compton's town center, Mount Auburn Cemetery was originally set on seventy-two acres purchased by the Massachusetts Horticultural Society. It was the first garden-like cemetery opened to the public in the United States. The meticulously maintained grounds enhanced a park of natural beauty and careful landscape design. Later described as "an earthly Elysian Field," Mount Auburn offered a place of peaceful repose for the dead, which in turn consoled the bereaved. At the cemetery's 1831 dedication attended by two thousand people, Associate Supreme Court Justice Joseph Story (himself a grieving parent) articulated the redirected, optimistic purpose of this resting place:

> As we sit down by their graves, we seem to hear the tones of their affection, whispering in our ears. We listen to the voice of their wisdom, speaking in the depths of our soul. We shed our tears but they are no longer the burning tears of agony. They relieve our drooping spirits. We return to the world and we feel

ourselves purer, and better, and wiser, from this communion with the dead.

A Festival of Churches

A thousand churches a year were built in America during Simmons' time. Each sect competed with different religious interpretations in this spiritually driven society. King's Chapel, a 1749 Georgian twelve-columned stone structure, served a conservative parish with a mixed Anglican-Unitarian liturgy. Located on the street where John would soon live, King's Chapel's articles of faith differed from the more liberal Brattle Street Unitarian congregation close to Dock Square that John and his family attended. Further along Tremont Street, Brimstone Corner was named for the fiery sermons delivered at the Park Street Church of conservative Congregationalists, which featured a two-hundred and seventeen-foot high steeple and was located across the street from Simmons' future home. A decade earlier, on July 4, 1831, twenty-three-year-old Samuel Smith performed a new song, "My Country Tis of Thee," at this church; the anthem-like hymn reflected the society's mix of patriotism with religion. On Tremont Street, across from the Boston Common, stood the Episcopal Cathedral Church of St. Paul. This Greek revival edifice served an elite congregation. The stern and elegant Doric-columned house of worship had its dedication ceremony in 1820, the year of John Jr.'s birth. Boston in the 1840s: a different creed on every corner.

133 Tremont Street

As the Simmons family needed more space and an address to reflect their changed station in life, John and Ann purchased land located next to St. Paul's from George Hayward on May 13, 1841. Ann Small Simmons decorated what became known as the Simmons Mansion, a five-story grand house on the northern side of the Episcopal church. By reputation, the Simmons Mansion had the finest interior finish of any other house in Boston, complete with Italian marble casings and rosewood doors. While this decade saw George Ripley experimenting with his utopian community of Brook Farm in West Roxbury, Bronson Alcott dragging his clan to Fruitlands, and Henry David Thoreau residing at Walden, John was uncharacteristically living in style at 133 Tremont. Unlike these progressive transcendentalists, John (usually a frugal man of simple needs) partook of some little luxuries. His fine sterling silverware and his delicate fine china set the tone for the elegance that graced his home. Here John could retreat after long days spent operating the largest clothing manufacturing company in New England, where thirty to forty percent of the population engaged in the trade.

Maid Service

Fitting the family's new economic status, three servants (Elizabeth Conner, Mary Callahan and Ann Kiernan) were on staff and lived upstairs. These three women, all Irish immigrants, were critical to the smooth running of John and Ann's large household. They were listed in the 1850 census as thirty-six, twenty-six and fifteen years old. Mid-century wages for women like Elizabeth, Mary, and Ann would have been four dollars each per month, plus room and board. Typical staff for this kind of household included a cook, a parlor maid and a younger woman to do the cleaning and washing. As live-in help, they were almost always on call, with the exception of one afternoon off each week. As people in the nineteenth century used their homes as part-time sick rooms, delivery rooms and as places for wakes, these three women provided help beyond their daily tasks and duties required by social occasions. There was always plenty of heavy lifting to be done. For example, bath water had to be warmed on a stove in the basement and then carried up and down flights of stairs since bathing was done in bedrooms in metal tubs.

"Erin's Daughters," as these unmarried Irish female servants were later called, came to America in far greater numbers than other immigrant women. The ratio of Irish female to male immigrants was 1:1 compared with a 1:7 ratio for other ethnic immigrants. Emigrating from a society where they were predisposed to be self-supporting, Irish women often came to America without their families. One advantage to living with their employers was the free room and board. They were often given uniforms. Living expenses were minimal, and Irish maids often had more financial independence than many other immigrant women. Living without kin, they were freer to spend their own money; they were quick to study the norms and customs of their wealthy American employers. These benefits could offset the loneliness, hard work and class ridicule their group may also have experienced.

By custom and for economic reasons, Irish women married later than other women so, like the early mill girls (employed to save dowry money), the Irish seized the benefits of work in the servant class. At the same time, native and other immigrant women chose to be needlewomen or factory workers rather than servants because by virtue of the factory work schedule, they would have evenings off. These women wanted to meet men and to live with their families before and after they married. Indeed, native born Protestant women often chose not to be servants, because in their culture there was a social stigma attached to living as a servant in a non-related man's house. Despite the supply of domestic service jobs available in the United States in the 1840s, only five percent of the free white population was employed in this way.

Employers favored Irish immigrants over other immigrant women as servants because they spoke English, albeit with an accent. Statistics show Irish women were a particularly "chaste group" with lower illegitimate birthrates at the time. Irish Catholic women's authority figures were priests who stressed abstinence and self-control. For Protestant employers the downside of employing Irish-American staff was the unexpectedly long training period needed to teach country girls the domestic sciences of city living.

Ann's Additional Responsibilities

As John's fortune rose, his wife Ann's work increased, but she redirected her energies toward a more varied daily existence. Finer foods, better furniture, and a bigger house to care for demanded much of a wife's time. Women of Ann's social status were expected to serve more elaborate meals than in previous generations, which would have required more planning and purchasing on Ann's part. New delicacies were available courtesy of S.S. Pierce, the fine foods store on the corner of Court and Tremont Streets, a business strategically located near Beacon Hill and the West End. Their stock included imported items brought to Boston on merchant ships and local fare like creamed corn—packaged for the first time in metal cans. Products were delivered in wheelbarrows to upper class customers who now cooked on stoves, far safer and more convenient than the open hearths Ann toiled over as a girl. In addition to food, a variety of social pastimes was expected. The family enjoyed playing music; John Jr.'s flute survives to this day.

Another essential element was refined and stately household accoutrements—John's silver service and his fine china remain intact, reflecting the elegant taste of his pretty wife. The Simmons family experienced material good fortune. Nevertheless, sorrow accompanied them to their mansion since Lorenzo, the Simmons' second son, died of consumption in February 1841, shortly before the purchase of the land on which their elegant home eventually stood.

Consumption

Tuberculosis, referred to as consumption in the 1840s, is an infectious disease caused by mycobacterium. It was rampant from 1830 to 1850. Before the era of antibiotics, the mortality rate of those with active disease was greater than fifty percent, especially affecting young adults. Symptoms of active tuberculosis are chronic cough, fever, night sweats and weight loss; hence the term "consumption." Its infection rate was highest among sedentary workers employed in cramped, poorly ventilated rooms. For this reason, farmers laboring outdoors were less susceptible. An infected patient in that era might infect ten to fifteen people a year through his coughing and sneezing, although unlike smallpox, tuberculosis wasn't proven to be contagious until 1869. The first sanatoriums to isolate the infected were not built until the 1870s, and in 1882 Dr. Robert Koch proved tuberculosis was a bacterial disease by isolating the organism responsible for it. These discoveries came far too late for poor Lorenzo Simmons.

Consumption's victims lost their thirst and appetite. For this reason, they "wasted away" and became pale. Consumption was called "the romantic disease" by those not suffering its effects. Bleeding, blistering, and purging were the only medical options at that time. A generation after Lorenzo's death, in Emily Dickinson's community of Amherst, Massachusetts, as George Mamunes reports in *"So Has a Daisy Vanished": Emily Dickinson and Tuberculosis,* six percent of TB victims died in the first week, seven percent in the first month, sixteen percent within three months and seventy-one percent after that. People sometimes lived for years with the disease. Some even considered it a "good death" because the disease's duration provided time to settle one's affairs. In New England, a quarter of the deaths before the Civil War were caused by tuberculosis. Many novels like Dumas' *La Dame aux Camellias* and Hugo's *Les*

Miserables include stories of consumption. Ralph Waldo Emerson's first wife Ellen's entire family was wiped out by this then incurable illness.

How long Lorenzo suffered is not known, but it is easy to imagine the pain Ann and John endured. To lose a child, so young and so full of promise must have emotionally burdened everyone in the family. Often, when a family member had consumption, relatives would take turns staying up to attend the sick; they were given the name "night watchers," and sadly, because of prolonged close contact they often shared their relative's fate.

The Family Responds

Two years later, in 1843, Simmons' eldest son, John Jr., age twenty-three, married Martha Parker Vinton. Unitarian minister Samuel Lothrop officiated at the ceremony. Martha was the daughter of a Washington Street confectionary shop owner, which indicated John Jr. married within his class. Two years later, Martha bore a son, John III. Devastatingly, when John III was only a year old, his father, too, died of tuberculosis in Cuba on April 4, 1846.

Perhaps his younger brother Lorenzo had infected John Jr. Perhaps in the close quarters of the manufacturing business John Jr. had caught this disease. How he got tuberculosis we will never know, but wealthy New Englanders did go to Cuba when they were unwell. New England merchants were familiar with that island since it supplied sugar, molasses and coffee, and the hilly parts of Cuba were thought favorable for health restoration. Some believed the winds could blow diseases away. Regardless, the warmer Caribbean climate attracted the ill in search of respite.

Despite his growing business success, John Simmons suffered personal loss with the premature deaths of his two eldest sons. His two daughters, Mary Ann and Alvina, would add to John's heartache as well.

Timeline 1795-1810

	1795	1800	1805	1810
UNITED STATES HISTORY	George Washington 1789-1797 John Adams 1797-1801	Thomas Jefferson 1801-1809		James Madison 1809-1817 War of 1812 (1812-1814)
CLOTHING MANUFACTURING HISTORY	Clothing sewn by hand at home or in tailor shops for the wealthy Cloth is handmade or imported from Europe	Locally manufactured materials	Customers buy on credit and negotiate prices	Francis Cabot Lowell begins Boston Manufacturing Company in Waltham 1814 John Simmons apprentices as a tailor at 15 Ann St. Boston 1814-1818
JOHN SIMMONS HISTORY	John Simmons is born in Little Compton, R.I. 1796 Ann Small is born in Provincetown, MA 1797	John learns to hunt and fish	John attends Peaked Top School in Little Compton, RI	John's brother George dies at sea 1814 John journeys to Boston in 1814 John apprentices with his brother Cornelius 1814

Timeline 1815-1830

	1815	1820	1825	1830
UNITED STATES HISTORY	James Munroe 1817-1825	John Quincy Adams 1825-1829		Andrew Jackson 1829-1837
	"Era of Good Feelings" 1817 Mass General Hospital cornerstone laid 1818	Missouri Compromise 1820	Erie Canal opens 1825 Quincy Market opens 1826 Perkins School for the Blind 1829	"The Liberator" 1831 Mass Temperance Society 1833
CLOTHING MANUFACTURING HISTORY	John sets up shop at 14 Ann St. Boston 1818	Standard tape measure invented 1820 John Simmons becomes early adopter of ready-to-wear clothing for men 1820s-1850s	John moves business to 51 North Market St. New store look features window displays	Protectionist tariffs Cotton production increases
JOHN SIMMONS HISTORY	John marries Ann Small in Boston October 1818 Daughter Mary Ann is born 1819 Family lives at 48 Ann St. Boston	Son John Jr. is born 1820 Son Lorenzo is born 1822 Daughter Alvina is born 1824	Son Theodore is born and dies 1829 Son Theodore II is born 1829 Family moves to 17 Staniford St. Boston	

| 1815 | 1820 | 1825 | 1830 |

Timeline 1835-1850

	1835	1840	1845	1850
UNITED STATES HISTORY		Martin Van Buren 1837-1841	James Polk 1845-1849	Zachary Taylor 1849-1850
		John Tyler 1841-1845		Millard Fillmore 1850-1853
	Broadcloth mob attacks Wm. Lloyd Garrison 1835 Depression of 1837	Margaret Fuller's Conversations 1842 Dorothea Dix lobbies for mentally ill 1843	Texas added to Union 1845 War with Mexico 1846-1848 First ether at MGH 1846 Seneca Falls Convention 1848	Fugitive Slave Act 1850 Kansas-Nebraska Act nullifies Missouri Compromise 1854
CLOTHING MANUFACTURING HISTORY		"Oak Hall" Established by George Simmons 1842 First use of hard-sell advertising in clothing industry Fixed pricing established	John Simmons uses RR's to send sales force west and south Elias Howe (inventor of sewing machine) tests product at Simmons' shop John declines purchase 1846	Simmons Block opens located on Congress, Water and Devonshire St. 1850 Lily (Women's Magazine) introduces bloomers 1851 Isaac Singer patents continuous stitch sewing Sewing machine wars between Singer and Howe ended 1854
JOHN SIMMONS HISTORY	Bennoni Simmons, John's father, dies 1835 Simmons buys plot for his family at Mt. Auburn Cemetery 1837	Son Lorenzo dies at age 19 1841 The Simmons Family moves to mansion 133 Tremont St. Boston 1841 Daughter Mary Ann elopes 1842 Son John Jr. marries Martha Vinton 1843 Dorothea Dix meets Abraham Simmons 1844	First Grandchild John III born 1845 Son John Jr. dies in Cuba 1846 Daughter Alvina elopes with Edward White 1847	Granddaughter Anna White born 1850 Son Theodore marries Harriet Jackson 1850 Granddaughter Ella born 1851 Grand daughter Harriet born 1852 Ella dies 1853 Grandson John III dies 1854

1835	1840	1845	1850

Timeline 1855-1870

	1855	1860	1865	1870
UNITED STATES HISTORY	Franklin Pierce 1853-1857 James Buchanan 1857-1861	Abraham Lincoln 1861-1865		Ulysses Grant 1869-1877 Andrew Johnson 1865-1869
UNITED STATES HISTORY	No Nothing Party 1856 Meeting to save the Union at Faneuil Hall 1859	Civil War 1861-1865 Vassar College Incorporated 1861 MIT-1861 Morrill Land Grant establishes State Colleges 1862	Lincoln assassinated in 1865 Reconstruction Stanton and Anthony start National Women's Suffrage Association 1869	Great Chicago Fire 1871 Great Boston Fire 1872 Boston University opens all divisions to female students in 1872
CLOTHING MANUFACTURING HISTORY	John Simmons invests in real estate with manufacturing profits 1857 John Simmons retires from clothing business 1858	John Simmons buys land at 1,2, and 3 Arlington St. Uniform production for Civil War	German Jews expand clothing manufacturing trade Standardized measurements for men's clothing begin based on Civil War statistics 1865	John Simmons leaves fortune to establish college for women 1870
JOHN SIMMONS HISTORY	Granddaughter Daisy born and dies 1855 Granddaughter Genevieve born and dies 1855 John's Mother Nancy dies 1855 Mary Ann divorces Ditson 1856 Son Theodore II dies1858 Wife Ann paralyzed 1858	Wife Ann dies May, 1861 John continues real estate acquisitions	John Simmons makes his will endowing Simmons College 1867	John Simmons adds codicil to will 1870 John Simmons dies of kidney disease in Little Compton RI 1870 Daughter Mary Ann marries William Buffum 1871 Fire destroys income producing properties 1872

Timeline 1875-1890

	1875	1880	1885	1890
UNITED STATES HISTORY	James Garfield 1881-1881 Rutherford Hayes 1877-1881	Chester Arthur 1881-1885	Benjamin Harrison 1889-1893 Grover Cleveland 1885-1889, 1893-1897	
	Smith College opens 1875 Wellesley College opens 1875		Mt Holyoke College awards first Bachelor degrees 1888	Radcliffe College incorporated 1893
CLOTHING MANUFACTURING HISTORY	Lord and Taylor sells first ready-to-wear for women 1870-1880	Clothing manufacturer Paul Tulane gives $2M to college in New Orleans 1882	More complicated women's clothing still made by hand (not mass produced)	No womens clothing for sale in Sears Roebuck Catalog 1894
JOHN SIMMONS HISTORY	Trustees mortgage land to rebuild Simmons College endowment	Nephew George Simmons dies 1882	Daughter Alvina dies in Boston 1886 Daughter Mary Ann dies in Wiesbaden Germany 1887 Dorothea Dix leaves funds for Simmons Scholars 1887 John's Lawyer Benjamen Brooks dies 1887	Son-in-law and trustee of will Edward White dies 1891
	1875	1880	1885	1890

Timeline 1895-1900

	1895	**1900**			
UNITED STATES HISTORY	William McKinley 1897-1901	Theodore Roosevelt 1901-1909			
	Simmons College incorporated 1899	Simmons College opens 1902			
CLOTHING MANUFACTURING HISTORY					
JOHN SIMMONS HISTORY	Simmons College named for founder 1899	William Buffum last son-in-law dies 1901 John's friend and Trustee Joseph Sawyer dies 1901			

1895   **1900**

Alvina Simmons White

*Alvina Simmons White (1824-1886) appears reserved in this family
album photograph. What could have been on her mind?*

Photo courtesy of Little Compton Historical Society.

63

Edward White

Despite an initial bad beginning, Alvina's husband, Edward White, became a valued son-in-law to John Simmons and was a trustee of John's will.

Photo courtesy of Little Compton Historical Society.

Mary Ann Simmons Ditson Buffum

Mary Ann Simmons Ditson Buffum (1819-1887), John's oldest child, was the most traveled of his children, and she experienced dramatic personal upheavals—and great love—throughout her life.

Photo courtesy of Little Compton Historical Society.

Buffum Jewelry

This gold and amber necklace in the "archaeological revival style" was purchased by Mary Ann's second husband, William Arnold Buffum, in Rome, Italy in approximately 1880. He later donated this piece and others to the Museum of Fine Arts in Boston.

Photograph ©October 2014 courtesy of the Museum of Fine Arts, Boston.

CHAPTER FIVE: DUCATS AND DAUGHTERS

Genius without education is like silver in the mine.
~Benjamin Franklin

Alvina Elopes

Shortly after her brother John's death, Alvina, Ann and John's younger daughter, eloped at age twenty-three. She went off with Edward A. White, a handsome, dark-haired, dark-eyed tailor from Washington Street, and married in Boston on March 3, 1847. John was initially very displeased by this union. Was it class, temperament, religious difference, or perhaps a prior marriage by White that made John disapprove of their union? Simmons College historian Kenneth Mack reports that John was disappointed by the lack of social advancement by his children. What dreams did he have for Alvina that were abandoned because of her relationship with White?

Despite her father's fortune, and as a woman in 1847, few options were available to Alvina. No New England college would admit women. She could not hold public office; indeed, she could not even vote. Once married, she could not keep her own name or her own property. She could only wear dresses and was expected to don a modest hair covering in public. A woman speaking in front of groups was considered rude. By custom, she could not seek employment in her father's business. However, a few brave women tried to circumvent the status quo through education and reform movements. In contrast to Alvina's mainstream lifestyle, alternative progressive women had a few other options.

Mount Holyoke

Would Alvina's life have been different if expectations were raised for her gender? What if she had attended Mary Lyon's Mount Holyoke Seminary? This South Hadley, Massachusetts women's preparatory school was founded in 1837 by an ambitious, effective fund-raiser, a teacher who believed young women over seventeen should have the same educational opportunities as their male counterparts. At that time, there were one-hundred and twenty colleges for men in the country; only Oberlin College in Ohio, founded in 1833, admitted women. Lyons chose to call her school a "seminary" rather than a "college" because the concept of women attending college was too threatening, too scandalous for that time. With a nod to the norms of female roles, Lyons insisted her students do the domestic work their institution needed, thereby keeping tuition costs low.

Lucy Stone

A famous 1839 graduate of Mount Holyoke, Lucy Stone was six years older than Alvina and lived a very different life. Lucy later completed her studies at Oberlin College with honors with the class of 1847. She became an abolitionist speaker, a radical expelled by her church. Marrying in 1855, Lucy kept her maiden name and bore a daughter at age thirty-nine. After the Civil War, Lucy supported male Negro suffrage over women's but later served on the board of the American Woman Suffrage Association, a group more conservative than Elizabeth Cady Stanton and Susan B. Anthony's National Woman's Suffrage Association. Lucy was an editor of the *Woman's Journal* and when she died at age seventy-five in 1893, she was the first woman to be cremated in New England. Lucy was a woman who spoke her mind. Perhaps John Simmons was aware of Lucy Stone and the choices she made—and how those choices affected the fledging nation.

13 West Street

In her early twenties, living at her parents' home, did Alvina know her neighbors, the Peabody sisters? Two blocks away at 13 West Street, steps from the Simmons mansion, Elizabeth Palmer Peabody, a multilingual translator of Goethe, ran the West Street Bookshop, a meeting spot popular with Boston's intellectuals. Inspired by William Ellery Channing at the Federal Street Unitarian Church and an admirer of Theodore Parker, an abolitionist clergyman, Elizabeth Peabody was the first woman to publish books in the United States. Although she never married, she was an early advocate of children's autonomy, later writing in support of kindergartens for disadvantaged children in America. When Sophia Peabody, Elizabeth's youngest sister, fell ill, she went to Cuba to recuperate, just as John Simmons Jr. would later do. Sophia would marry author Nathaniel Hawthorne. Middle sister Mary would marry Horace Mann, the liberal reformer who advocated for women's education as well. Both weddings took place in the back room of Elizabeth's bookstore in the Simmons family's neighborhood.

Margaret Fuller

At this same address, while Alvina was in her teens, at the West Street Bookshop, Margaret Fuller, originally from Cambridgeport, began a series of "Conversations" for women who were barred from higher education. Fuller was the most famous free thinking female leader of her day. She prized self-definition over community-assigned identity. Two hundred women attended Fuller's lectures, twenty-five at a time, committing to thirteen-week sessions once a week from noon to two. Participants listened to Fuller lecture on subjects such as education, ethics and culture. These talks were followed by an audience response time wherein women were actively encouraged to air their thoughts and questions aloud. When Alvina was nineteen-years old, Margaret Fuller wrote the essay "The Great Lawsuit. Man versus Men. Woman vs. Women." Did Alvina ever read, appreciate, or echo the key point of Margaret Fuller's essay:

> By Man I mean both man and woman; these are two halves of one thought….I believe that the development of the one cannot be effected without that of the other. My highest wish is that the truth should be distinctly and rationally apprehended, and the

conditions of life and freedom recognized as the same for the daughter and the sons of time, twin exponents of a divine thought.

Regarding women's work, Fuller suggested a variety of jobs be available to women. "Let them be sea captains, if they will," she wrote.

Reformers

In 1848, a group of political activists gathered, hoping to redress the inequities of women in this "land of liberty." On July 19th and 20th, in upstate New York, three-hundred people, including forty men, gathered for a Women's Rights Conference at Seneca Falls. The town was then a prosperous manufacturing site forty-five miles west of Syracuse with links to the Erie Canal. Its industrial sector specialized in the construction of metal and fire-fighting equipment. New concepts of gender relations followed the expanding economy. Women's educational opportunities expanded as the region grew more prosperous. Critical thinking skills followed. At this inaugural meeting, one-hundred men and women signed the Seneca Falls Declaration, modeled after the Declaration of Independence. Elizabeth Cady Stanton, a tireless lifelong women's rights advocate, was overjoyed by both positive and negative press. Stanton explained: "The publicity…will start women thinking and men too; and when men and women think about a new question the first step in progress is taken." Newspaper accounts of the convention were twenty-nine percent favorable in describing the event, forty-two percent opposed, and twenty-eight percent neutral.

After Seneca Falls

Two years later, seven Seneca Falls veterans organized The National Women's Rights Convention, which was held in Worcester, Massachusetts in October of 1850. Worcester, then a wealthy manufacturing town, was the center of many reform movements. Located mid-state, it made a perfect geographic site, and its constituents embodied prevailing liberal philosophies and ideas. Reformers at the convention asked that the word "male" be stricken from the Massachusetts constitution, that women be allowed to vote, and that greater opportunities for higher education be given to women. By 1855, Massachusetts passed a law that permitted women to keep their property after marriage; at the same time, Massachusetts became the first state to allow women to keep their own wages. With such swift progressive legislation, who could have imagined national suffrage for women would not be accomplished for another seventy years!

Alvina's Story Continues

Shortly after Alvina and Edward White eloped, John Simmons, nineteenth century paterfamilias, reconciled with his son-in-law and daughter. John Simmons took Edward into his firm, and he gave the couple a beautiful home at 226 Tremont Street on the corner of Eliot Street, a few blocks down from his own residence. Edward White later became a trustee of his father-in-law's will. John Simmons wisely embraced Alvina and Edward; through them, John became a grandfather to Anna Simmons White, the joy of his later life.

Family history and ancestral charts describe Anna Simmons White as an only child. However, a photo of a younger Alvina White in a Simmons family album presently located at Little Compton Historical Society pictures a light-haired little girl labeled "Alvina White—adopted daughter of E. A. White." Yet the City of Boston Birth Registry records the younger Alvina's birth at 226 Tremont Street to her parents, Edward and Alvina White on January 11, 1857. In both the 1860 and 1870 census reports, this Alvina is still living with her parents, her older sister Anna and various Irish domestics. The label "adopted daughter" gives one pause. A mystery remains about the younger Alvina's history and her omission in the family's records and inheritances.

While John's daughter Alvina may have been more traditional than radical, perhaps she agreed with, learned from, understood, and appreciated the reformers and great thinkers of her time. Later in life, Alvina would create an autograph book for Anna Simmons White in which she collected the names of the following luminaries: Horace Mann (progressive education); Theodore Parker (an abolitionist who in 1851 invited a woman to speak from his pulpit); Senator Edward Everett (a featured Gettysburg speaker); Edwin Booth (John Wilkes Booth's actor brother); and even a progressive, controversial wit, playwright Oscar Wilde. These signatories were people who spoke for themselves by way of cultural critique. That Alvina would prize their names suggests her own awareness of history and her admiration for their positive leadership and talent.

Mary Ann's Story

John's daughter Mary Ann, however, lived a radically different life than that of her younger sister. Years earlier in 1842, John's eldest child was studying in New York, a state which had incorporated twenty-two female seminaries. There, the twenty-three-year old met Englishman George L. Ditson. The two were married without the knowledge or consent of the bride's father on November 13, 1842 by a Doctor Spring. The couple traveled to Europe and then on to Cuba where they lived for a few years. Then suddenly, John Simmons, a homebody—whose usual travels ranged from Boston to Little Compton and back—sped down to that island and whisked his daughter home. What happened? Was Ditson abusive? A failure? A fraud? A swindler? What horrible crime required John's intervention? Or was John an overbearing father? Court records later report Ditson had abandoned his wife in Cuba "in a feeble and emaciated condition, without any provision." John brought Mary Ann back to Boston.

In 1850, George returned to his wife and lived with Mary Ann at her parents' home on Tremont Street. He was employed in the textile trade. But once again, in 1853, George abandoned Mary Ann and left for Europe saying he "did not care a damn for Boston or any body in it."

Divorce

Following Ditson's departure, Mary Ann Simmons Ditson lived in Rhode Island for three years, perhaps seeking to avoid a scandal in Boston. On July 26, 1856, *The Newport Mercury* ran a request by the Clerk of the Supreme Court of Rhode Island addressed to George Ditson "residing in parts unknown" announcing that Mary Ann Ditson of Little Compton was petitioning to dissolve her marriage. In the August 1856 "Report of Cases Argued and Determined in the Supreme Court of Rhode Island," Mary Ann described Ditson as treating her "morosely and unkindly"; "he locked her up once in her chamber for making a purchase that displeased him." She even petitioned the court to take back her maiden name. She divorced Ditson (a rare event in pre-Civil War society), and at age fifty-two, shortly after her parents died, she married William Arnold Buffum.

William was the son of Arnold Buffum, a Providence hat manufacturer better known as a prominent abolitionist in Rhode Island, and Sarah Gould Buffum. Mary Ann's second husband had been United States Consul to Trieste from 1854-1859. Her sister-in-law, Elizabeth Buffum Chace, was an eminent leader in the women's rights movements, as well as an advocate for prison reform. Mary Ann and William resided in Boston, first at the Simmons Mansion, then at 222 Beacon Street, and later at 56 Commonwealth Avenue. With Mary Ann, William Buffum amassed a large and valuable collection of amber objects which included a casket of ebony with ivory and silver male and female caryatids, which he donated to the Museum of Fine Arts, Boston in 1901. Mary Ann and William had a childless marriage of sixteen years. She died in Wiesbaden, Germany, a spa town, in 1887.

Curiously, Mary Ann kept trinkets from her first marriage—found only after her death at age sixty-eight. Nonetheless, George Ditson had a scarring effect on the heart and purse strings of John Simmons. In his will, written more than a decade after his daughter's divorce, Simmons emphatically and unconditionally stated that George was never to see a penny from the Simmons estate.

Even with the gender restrictions put upon them by society, Alvina and Mary Ann had an easier life than working class women. John Simmons was able to use his power and influence to protect his daughters. But what of other women, such as seamstresses, lacking such compassionate support?

Needlewomen

In John Simmons' day, almost all women learned to sew. In the majority of lower- and middle-class households, wives and sisters made and mended their family's attire, but once the industrial revolution began, many men moved from farm to factory. As male workers migrated to the city, they needed a change of wardrobe to suit their new labors. Women were hired to meet the new demand for ready-to-wear clothing.

The sewers called needlewomen ranged from independent day laborers glad to make extra money to exploited piece workers at the mercy of the marketplace. Needlewomen who sewed and mill girls making textiles both shared twelve-hour workdays. The mill girls worked from six o'clock in the morning to six o'clock in the evening. Employers resisted when the Lowell Female Reform Association, a precursor of unions, requested a ten-hour workday, and they countered by hiring Irish immigrants with less wage-bargaining power.

Needlewomen differed from their contemporary sisters in the Lowell mills—they did not live in community boarding houses, nor did they have the educational and cultural opportunities mill girls were given early on. *The Lowell Offering* was a journal written by and for women. In contrast, sewers worked by themselves with less supervision. They were seasonal, not full-time, workers. Since they worked at home rather than in factories, these women might be expected to do additional household tasks during their sewing hours. Just as slaves were responsible for low cotton production costs, needlewomen's work at low pay was a key factor in the huge profits made by King Cotton manufacturing.

Who were these women? Where did they come from? John Simmons employed women from Roxbury and the South End of Boston. He employed war widows from the War of 1812. He hired immigrant women and farmers' wives who sewed in the winter season. John Simmons sometimes delivered the piece goods cut by his male tailors back in Boston to the women confined to their homes. Entering their living spaces, this forthright clothing manufacturer saw with his own eyes the impoverished living conditions of many in his female workforce. Over time he observed their skills, recognized their talents, appreciated their work ethic and learned of their personal hardships. Perhaps he mourned the job applicants who were too unskilled for him to hire, and he must have recognized that these women had often lost their male providers through no fault of their own. In this patriarchal society, widowhood, business failures, abandonment, and a spouse's alcoholism or abusive behavior often played a role in making many women desperate for paid work.

Given the cultural restrictions of the times, what were a poor woman's options? Was it better to beg, steal, take charity, or starve? Sewing was more socially acceptable compared to those options. Although these women were at the mercy of their male bosses, John Simmons had a reputation as a kind-hearted, self-made man, hailed in business guides as honorable in his business practices. Word of mouth about John's treatment of employees must have been an effective employment recruitment tool.

In Simmons' day, ready-to-wear outfits were designed exclusively for men. Why? Because men's fashions were simpler and therefore easier and less costly to produce. The earliest women's ready-to-wear items included wraps and comfortable coats. Due to its intricacy, women's ready-to-wear developed much later than men's, not flourishing until the twentieth century. Clothing historians such as Beth Harris, editor of *Famine and Fashion: Needlewomen in the Nineteenth Century,* have suggested that most seamstresses were invisible to the public, and some were stigmatized because of their labor. While sewing work provided women with extra income, at times their husbands resented their economic liberation. How could a father or husband get his daughter or wife to work for him unpaid once she had a taste of financial independence? This situation continues even today. Since manufacturing business owners knew their profit margins were due to the work of seamstresses, they wanted to keep these women under their control. Some men feared that if women could negotiate their way in the workplace, perhaps they would begin to see their marriages as negotiable contracts as well. Perhaps some men felt threatened by women's independence, perceiving it as a fissure in the social structure. Women were often considered ornamental, not as contributing members of America's growing economy.

Some wealthy women feared their less-privileged working sisters. They were encouraged by social norms to spend their energy and talents on home goods and fashion—to have more clothes reflected improved status, even as it drew women's attention away from full independence. To enforce the idea of a refined existence and to purchase the clothes reflecting social status, wealthy woman were encouraged to visit dressmakers in their leisure time. Fostering guilt at the overconsumption of now less expensive custom-made clothes (compared with their mother and grandmother's wardrobes), some magazines depicted women reacting with pity or scorn toward the very needlewomen who made their purchases possible.

By contrast, a few middle-class women joined sewing circles and made clothing for the working class women who sewed for a living. Historian Michael Zakim, author of *Ready-Made Democracy:*

A History of Men's Dress in the American Republic, tells of one group, The Ladies' Sewing Society of Baltimore, which sewed once a week at the donated factory space where their charity recipients worked.

The World of Letters and Needlewomen

Nineteenth century literature is filled with scenes of this social chasm that cast both rich and poor women in bad light. Vain, narcissistic wealthy women are portrayed in middle-class magazines as foils for isolated, overworked, exploited poor seamstresses. Elites pitied these waifs their bondage and humiliation. They advocated charity or state-sponsored relief instead of more lasting political, economic and organizational reform.

John Simmons may have favored charity himself in the 1830s. He was a member of the Brattle Street Church, known for supplying anonymous gifts of clothing to the poor. Years of experience later, John would reach a more systemic answer to eliminating female poverty.

Some social critics, however, identified customers as the real villains in this nineteenth century market. *The New York Tribune* (July 31, 1851) printed these lines from "Song of the Shirt" describing a labor-intensive garment sewed exclusively by female labor:

> "O, men, with sisters dear!
> O, men, with mothers and wives!
> It is not linen you're wearing out,
> But human creatures lives."

The Midnight Queen, or: Leaves from New York Life (1853) asks consumers:

> Now gentle and comfortable people, who smack your lips as you say—'Any one that is not idle and improvident can get along; the idle, the improvident, the criminal only are poor'—will you tell us the particular sin of this girl-woman, who is now digging her grave with her needle?

In 1872 Louisa May Alcott published *Work*, a novel in which her Christ-like heroine, Christine, seeks job opportunities permitted to her gender: servant, actress, governess, companion, nurse, and seamstress. In this final occupation a character threatens: "I'll do Slop work [sew clothes] and starve." Alcott responded to those choices by giving Christine's story a socially just conclusion—her heroine inherits her former farm home and lives surrounded by the workingwomen she'd encountered and admired along her employment journey.

Boston Marriages

In the nineteenth century, because of social restrictions, single females seldom lived apart from their families. Upper-class Brahmin women sometimes preferred life with their same-sex friends. Some were unwilling to risk the disappointment of a traditional marriage in which women's second-class status and male privilege was the law of the land. Using family funds or personal income (from teaching, writing, and art work) some of these women lived together in long-term romantic and sexual relationships called "Boston Marriages," named for their location and relatively long-lasting committed partnerships. The concept was introduced in the literary world by Henry James in his 1886 novel *The Bostonians*. According to the History Project's *Improper Bostonians: Lesbian and Gay History from the Puritans to Playland*, James' characters were based on his sister Alice's relationship with Katharine Peabody Loring, which he described as "a devotion so perfect and generous.... a gift so rare.... that to brush it aside would be almost an act of impiety." Such women referred to themselves as women in romantic friendships and today would likely self-identify as lesbians. Free of husbands, children and attendant household responsibilities, they developed their own network of culture, intellectual activity and emotional support.

For example, Boston born Charlotte Cushman (1816-1876), a popular versatile actor who played more than thirty male roles including Romeo, had consecutive relations with two other famous sculptors, Emma Stebbins (1815-1882) and Harriet Hosmer (1830-1908). Relationships between less affluent women with such desires are not prominently recorded as less affluent people would have been of little interest to the general population, which may account for the lack of documentation. Presumably they made their own arrangements as best they could. After new institutions like women's colleges and social clubs were formed in the later part of the century, women's independence grew and with it the capacity and power to take pleasure in one another's company.

The Sewing Machine

What made John Simmons' success unusual was that he earned most of his manufacturing fortune decades before the sewing machine was invented. While most people associate this invention with Isaac Singer, it was actually Elias Howe, a mechanic born in Spencer, Massachusetts, who was awarded the first sewing machine patent in 1846. Others had produced earlier design ideas, but Howe's concept featured a needle with the eye at the point, a lock stitch and an automatic feed. Surprisingly, few initial customers bought his product. Tailors and needlewomen feared the machine's labor-saving ability would put them out of work, much as today's assembly-line employees fear automation. As the sewing machine was a new invention requiring a large capital outlay in terms of construction, Howe priced his machine at three-hundred dollars. Clothing manufacturers could hire needlewomen at far less expense. So Howe, an unsuccessful salesman, went to England to peddle his new product.

In June of 1850, Isaac Singer was in Boston working on his own invention for carving printer's type at the machine shop of Orson P. Phelps. According to Harold Evans et al. in *They Made America*, Singer, like Howe, had no luck with buyers in the publishing world. Ironically, failing to see the similarities between his unpurchased product and that of Elias Howe, he judged the idle sewing machine he noticed at Phelps' shop with contempt. "What a devilish machine!" Singer reportedly exclaimed. "You want to do away with the one thing that keeps women quiet, their sewing?"

Despite his initial rejection of this invention, Singer made a needle design modification and started selling his product in New York. Singer's machines were pared down and sold for fifty dollars to individuals rather than clothing manufacturers. Returning from England, Howe came upon Singer selling his invention. Howe sued Singer and won his case, receiving five dollar royalties from Singer on each machine sold. Howe died in 1867 after serving the North in the Civil War. Singer continued his business on Mott Street selling twenty-five hundred machines in 1856 and thirteen thousand in 1860. Singer became a multi-millionaire, and he died in 1875, two years before the machine patent expired.

Interestingly, John Simmons had a chance to be an early investor in Howe's sewing machine. In 1846, Howe brought his invention to John Simmons and Company at Quincy Hall in Boston. According to the July 27, 1860 deposition in the records of Blatchford, Seward and Griswold, a New York law firm specializing in patent cases, George P. Clapp, a former Simmons employee, testified that Howe tried to sell his machine to Simmons fourteen years earlier. Howe staged a race at Simmons' business address: five of Simmons' "best and fastest" needlewomen sewed by hand against Howe at his sewing machine to see if the women or machine produced the best-sewn strips of cloth. Clapp was the judge. The machine was faster than the "girls," he noted and the machine work was "neatest and strongest." Of the "girls" Clapp said, "Their sewing was very good but the machine was better." Despite this experiment and business opportunity, Clapp reported, John Simmons did not purchase any of Howe's machines. Howe's three-hundred dollar product may have been too expensive for this bottom-line conscious manufacturer.

In other shops at later dates mass production of sewing machines drove their purchase price down. But the adoption of the sewing machine—like the cotton gin of an earlier time—only increased the workload for seamstresses. They were required to make more products in less time. The machine reduced clothing construction costs by eighty percent since sewing machines could work up to twenty times faster to accomplish the same tasks done by hand. The frock coat, which took 16.5 hours to make by hand, could be manufactured with a sewing machine in 2.5 hours. As a bonus, sewing machines created uniform stitches. Cost savings were once again passed on to the consumer with no extra rewards for seamstresses who had done the work.

The Beecher Solution

How could these women ever escape their employment dilemmas? Catharine Beecher worked on this problem. As the bright, first-born, never-married daughter of clergyman Lyman Beecher and sister to Henry Ward Beecher, Catharine struggled to give significant purpose to her own life. She realized life was precious. She believed thrift and hard work and self-denial could lead to a more secure life. She proposed a radical solution in 1851. In *The True Remedy for the Wrongs of Woman*, the elder sister of Harriet Beecher Stowe proposed this unorthodox solution: establish women's colleges! First, Beecher suggested these colleges should be housed in large towns and big cities to create urban centers where females could have voice and influence. Second, she believed these colleges should be endowed with funds to train women as teachers so that women could have worthy, prestigious careers on their own. Third, Beecher argued that women's colleges would prepare women for their "true professions" as educators and as homemakers.

In the year of her book's publication, John Simmons was in his early fifties and actively operating his large, profitable organization with his one surviving son, Theodore. Years later, Beecher's *True Remedy* proposal would surface in Simmons' affairs. But for the present, it was business as usual at John Simmons and Son.

John Simmons III

John III (1845-1854) was a year old when his father, John Jr. died. Yet this darling young boy and only grandson of John Simmons is pictured in a pleasant scene in a portrait in the Simmons College Archives.

Anna Simmons White Rowe

This picture shows Alvina's daughter, Anna Simmons White Rowe, as a baby. Anna's image appears in a brooch worn by her grandmother, Ann Small Simmons.

Photo courtesy of Simmons College Archives.

BLAKE, BIGELOW & CO.,

IMPORTERS OF

BROAD CLOTHS, CASSIMERES,

VESTINGS,

And every description of Clothiers' Goods,

CHAMBERS IN SIMMONS BLOCK,

Corner of Water and Congress Streets,

Simmons Block

The Simmons Block on Congress and Water streets in downtown Boston was a four-story plus attic space sales and manufacturing facility with rental units built in 1850, presumably as a legacy for John's youngest son, Theodore Augustus II. Note the sign "T.A. Simmons and Co." on the right side of the building.

Photo courtesy of The Boston Athenaeum.

CHAPTER SIX: IS IT FAIR?

*The heart of a fool is in his mouth, but the mouth of a wise man
is in his heart.*
> ~Benjamin Franklin

Happy Days

On January 6, 1850, the Feast of Epiphany, two major events occurred which made John Simmons a happy man. His younger daughter, Alvina, gave birth to her first child, Anna Simmons White, and on the same day his only surviving son, Theodore Augustus, was married. Just shy of twenty-one, Theodore wed Harriet W. Jackson, the daughter of a wealthy soap manufacturer from Roxbury, Massachusetts. As his deceased older brother John had done before him, Theodore chose a wife from the manufacturing class.

The United States Census of 1850 reports clothing storeowner John Simmons' house on Tremont Street had a market value of $170,000. Thirty-two years after coming to Boston, John Simmons was one of the city's wealthiest men. To cement his success and ensure the future, in 1850 John Simmons built "The Simmons Block," a large building on the corners of Water, Congress and Devonshire Streets (presently the Post Office Square area), prime real estate in the antebellum metropolis. The ground floor of the building held retail shops. The next three floors and an attic space were used for clothing manufacturing and storage. All this expansion was executed by John with his partner Alvin Rose, who joined Simmons in 1846. John had also taken Theodore into his business. With fatherly pride, undoubtedly John anticipated his son would learn the trade and eventually take over the expanding ready-wear manufacturing operation. As evidence of his faith in his son, a drawing of the Simmons Block shows the sign "T. A. Simmons" prominently displayed on the storefront.

Simmons' business success continued. The April 29, 1850 *Salem Register* reported the positive news that John Simmons and Company made Cambridge City Guard uniforms "without exception, the cheapest, the neatest and yet the most showy of any in the state." Likewise, on May 9, 1851, a Boston newspaper editorialized:

> By invitation of the proprietors we paid a visit...to the extensive clothing establishment of Messrs. JOHN SIMMONS & Co., in Simmons Block, corner of Congress and Water streets. This new edifice is one of the most spacious and elegant in the city, being 50 feet in front, and over 150 in depth. The amount of business transacted at this establishment is almost incredible. Five stories are devoted to the various branches—salesroom, wareroom, work-room, &e. Twenty cutters are constantly employed in the building, and from seventy to eighty other persons, in the different departments. We were assured that the number of persons employed by this firm, in the city and country, is between four and five thousand. The enterprise and industry of Mr. Simmons have thus built up an establishment second, we believe, to no other in the country.

William Lloyd Garrison

The positive review mentioned above appeared in *The Liberator*, the abolitionist newspaper founded and edited by William Lloyd Garrison in 1831; the newspaper's goal was to promote the immediate abolition of slavery, then a radical idea. At that time, the financial and mercantile community, including John Simmons, benefitted enormously from low-priced cotton picked and tended to by slaves laboring in Southern states. When Garrison, through his newspaper, questioned the system and demanded slaves be set free immediately, Southern slave-owning businessmen (later called "Lords of the Lash") were outraged by the Northerner's attack on their labor pool and key financial asset. They demanded that their Massachusetts business colleagues, the textile mill owners (later called "Lords of the Loom"), quiet this upstart Garrison. One Southern periodical warned, "grass will grow in the streets of Lowell [a partner mill city receiving their cotton] if strong measures were not taken against those fanatical wretches [abolitionists]." Most white people believed abolition would destroy the social order. Amos A. Phelps conducted a survey in 1831 of Unitarian ministers in eastern Massachusetts. Only one in eight had strong objections to slavery at that time. In October of 1835, a "broadcloth mob" (elite merchants—so called because of their upper-class garb) went to Garrison's office and roughed him up in a violent attempt to scare him away from his mission. Compassionate African Americans came to his rescue and helped him get away. The next day, John B. Vashon, a black abolitionist, presented Garrison with a new hat replacing the one he had lost in the scuffle. It would take years of violence, political failures and consistent lobbying to change many Yankee minds about the horrors of slavery. Few people have "road to Damascus" moments. Most minds are persuaded gradually over time.

One group of Garrison supporters formed the Anti-Slavery Sewing Circle, raising funds for immediate and complete abolition of slavery. As transcribed in *Antebellum Women: Private, Public, Partisan* by Carol Lasser and Stacey Robertson, and writing in the *Anti-Slavery Bugle* on January 22, 1847, Jane Elizabeth Hitchcock Jones asked:

> We have a system in our midst which robs mothers of their children, should not mothers labor earnestly for its overthrow? We have a system which robs wives of their husbands, should not wives be zealous to destroy it?~We have an institution that degrades and brutalizes woman, sells her for gold, destroys the virtuous emotions of her nature, should not woman ever be hostile to it, and strive to save her sex from so sad a fate?

The World Beyond Tremont Street

While prosperity was a hallmark for Simmons, many of those in the world outside his 133 Tremont Street mansion suffered relentless heartaches. In the 1840s, two thousand African Americans called Boston home. They lived on the lower slope of Beacon Hill on Belknap Street, which is now Joy Street, and on Cambridge Street near the Massachusetts General Hospital, and in the North End.

Black bachelors tended to reside in North End boarding houses close to their work as seamen, teamsters and dock workers. On Beacon Hill a typical African American family consisted of a married couple and two children, a number smaller than white families of the same time period.

The African Meeting House was nearby, home to the African Baptist Church. Parallel to the white community's outreach, the African Society sponsored temperance talks, self-improvement lectures and educational initiatives. Churches provided social and spiritual support to newcomers. From their pulpits came active encouragement for abolition and civil rights. Community leaders included Lewis Hayden, a Phillips Street clothing storeowner, Robert Morris, a well-regarded lawyer who also represented Irish immigrants, and Charles Lenox Redmond, an international speaker and debater on behalf of abolition. Black Bostonians were loyal residents of Massachusetts because the Commonwealth was more sympathetic than the federal government to their residential and legal status. While they went to segregated schools until 1855, free black males could vote in Massachusetts elections. Peter Howard's barbershop on Cambridge Street was a central station in the underground railroad. Senator Charles Sumner often visited Howard's business to gather abolition information. The Underground Railroad in Boston has many heroes—including the North End bachelors. Unfortunately, their names were rarely recorded given the illegality of their pursuits.

Until midcentury, African Americans saw the city as a refuge for personal and political freedom, a haven of community organized laborers, freedmen and women, as well as trained professionals who had apprenticed as lawyers and doctors. Since the Fugitive Slave Law of 1793 required the return of runaway slaves to slaveholders, Quakers, white abolitionists and freed blacks had tried by legal means to circumvent this law. But in 1842 George Latimer, an escaped slave, was arrested in Boston. After a failed attempt led by Henry G. Travey and fellow blacks to rescue him, blacks and whites rallied together for his release. Latimer's owner, James B. Gray, eventually accepted four hundred dollars collected by African Americans for Latimer's release. Community outrage yielded community action. Approximately 64,526 people signed a petition to the Massachusetts legislature to strengthen anti-slavery measures. In 1843, the Latimer Law was enacted, protecting the individual liberty of both blacks and whites. It forbade Massachusetts officials from apprehending runaway slaves. Supporters of the law hoped the legislation would make it too costly for slave owners to pursue runaways without local help.

However, in 1850 with California being admitted to the union as a free state, Senators Henry Clay of Kentucky and Daniel Webster of Massachusetts suggested a political compromise to appease the Southern states. To maintain the status quo (a balance of slave and free states) they proposed strengthening the Fugitive Slave Law, making it a federal crime to interfere with recapturing and returning runaways. Like all textile businesses, John's profited from slave labor in the South. Both his church and his community continued to have mixed opinions in the intersection of commerce and morality.

Slavery Matters in Boston

Just blocks from John's office, at the Boston Courthouse in 1851, a recaptured runaway slave, Shadrach Minkins, was held in custody. He was subsequently liberated by free African Americans and shuttled out of American jurisdiction to safety in Montreal. Two months later, escaped slave Thomas Sims was arrested, but this time a steadfast, white militia served as guards. Although the Boston Vigilance Committee, an abolitionist group, tried to rescue him, Sims was returned by ship to Georgia where he received thirty-nine lashes in a public square in Savannah on April 19, 1851. Sims later escaped from slavery during the Civil War.

In a similar case, Anthony Burns, a runaway slave from Alexandria, Virginia found employment with Mr. Coffin Pitts, a Boston clothing dealer. Yet in 1854 Burns was discovered, jailed, tried and sentenced. On the second of June, Burns was shackled and escorted by armed guards to a ship bound for Virginia. Onlookers sympathetic to Burns lined the route from the courthouse to the wharf. The Brattle Street Church, John's house of worship, rang its bells that day to protest Burns' return to bondage. That same month the Merchant's Exchange issued a petition signed by many of Boston's commercial elite for repeal of the brutal Fugitive Slave Law. Eventually, Pitts and the 12th Street Baptist Church in Boston were able to purchase Burns' freedom. He went on to Oberlin College and a Theological Seminary in Connecticut. He served as pastor of a Baptist church in St. Catharines, Ontario. He contracted tuberculosis and died at age twenty-nine in 1862.

Boston's merchants and manufacturers were motivated to protest the federal law not only on humanitarian grounds, but for practical reasons. These leaders believed that free labor, not slave labor, produced the best results for society as a whole. Embracing their own versions of the Protestant work ethic and Unitarian concepts of the perfectibility of mankind, Amos A. Lawrence (son of textile owner Amos Lawrence) and his supporters also believed that public education and democratic institutions would give all individuals the best chance at maximizing their potential—with the results to be shared by all in the commonwealth. Since these leaders had personally benefitted from the free-labor economy, they had complete faith in this system, but they were blind to the real inequities and harsh labor conditions their own employees sometimes experienced. The outcome of Anthony Burns' trial appalled the elites. Referring to the legal sentence imposed on Burns and the merchants' inability to gain justice for him, Amos A. Lawrence said "We went to bed one night, old fashioned, conservative, compromise Union Whigs and waked up stark mad abolitionists."

Cotton versus Conscience

What did John think of Amos A. Lawrence's appraisal of this Northern wake-up call? It is probable that John Simmons had been a member of the Whig party. Originally, this pro-business alliance supported modernization, education, and economic protections like tariffs on imported cloth. But by the 1850s, opposing beliefs about slavery divided the party into two factions: the Cotton Whigs and the Conscience Whigs, the former favoring social position, the latter social justice. Cotton Whigs expressed sympathy toward slaves yet they supported slave owners and their enterprises. Practical business owners like Abbott Lawrence and Nathan Appleton favored the status quo; they were conservatives who wanted to preserve the union and business transactions at all costs. Cotton Whigs supported territorial expansion and used talk of Southern secession as a political weapon.

On the other hand, Conscience Whigs like Ralph Waldo Emerson, Henry David Thoreau and Samuel Gridley Howe were anti-slavery. Conscience Whigs took the moral high road and sent funds to aid free-staters (emigrants from the East moving to territories hoping to make their land a free rather than a slave state). Conscience Whigs supported anti-slavery resolutions. They had been heavily influenced by religious reformers and liberal elites whose target audience, the middle class, was most approachable and amenable to issues of social progress.

Progressives

In Boston, John Simmons was surrounded by education advocates. One change agent was Horace Mann, a farmer's son from Franklin, Massachusetts who attended Brown University. Once a successful merchant with two small textile companies in Dedham,

Massachusetts, Mann re-ordered his priorities after the early death of his first wife, Charlotte. He became less involved in commerce, more in commonwealth. As chair of the Massachusetts Board of Education, he advocated education as a great social equalizer. He believed the state had paternal responsibilities to all its citizens, especially the poor, the ill and uneducated.

As a sign of changing times and an increased understanding of the need for education, in 1848, near the Simmons' home at the Tontine Crescent, the Boston Public Library was founded. As recorded in *The Hub: Boston Past and Present* by Thomas H. O'Connor, the writer Van Wyck Brooks later described the cultural atmosphere of that time, that place. "Boston, all New England," Brooks wrote, "respected learning. No New England boy was allowed to question that he was destined to succeed in life provided he knew enough: and Boston was determined that the boys and the girls and the blind and the insane as well, should have the opportunity to know enough." By midcentury, thanks to educational leaders from Massachusetts, American female literacy rates matched their male counterparts. The United States was the first country in the world to make this happen.

John and his son owned shares in The Boston Athenaeum, an independent library founded in 1807 with both painting and sculpture galleries at its 1849 Beacon Street location, a block up Park Street from the family home. One significant book on the shelves at the Athenaeum was *Uncle Tom's Cabin*. Written in 1852 by Harriet Beecher Stowe (sister of educational reformer Catharine Beecher) as a rebuttal to the hated and newly strengthened Fugitive Slave Law, which expanded the search parameters for fugitive slaves and criminalized any person aiding their escape, Stowe's anti-slavery novel sold ten thousand copies in a week. Reading this dramatic account of slavery was both an educational and emotional experience for those without firsthand knowledge of slavery. In the privacy of one's home, readers' hearts and minds were opened and persuaded against slavery through this enormously popular work of fiction.

Know Nothings

Not everyone was moved by or sympathetic to the hardships of others. During this period of social conflict that pitted slavery against abolition, and women's rights against the patriarchal status quo, an anti-immigration, pro-temperance party emerged as a reaction to the changing demographics in Massachusetts. As this group originated in secret as an anti-immigration, anti-Catholic body, members were encouraged to say, "I know nothing" when questioned about group activities. Later called the American Party, the Know Nothing Party's goal was to "eliminate Rome, Rum and Robbery."

As early as 1825, the average American over age fifteen was consuming seven gallons of alcohol a year, and alcoholism was a problem that various temperance movements hoped to correct. Abstinence pledgers were called teetotalers because they signed a 'T' after their names. The 'T' meant total abstinence. Such were the cultural issues that John Simmons observed and heard debated during his lifetime.

Unitarian Faith

Instead of joining the Know Nothings, John Simmons chose to be a member of a Unitarian church. It's fair to assume he approved of the values, history and leadership of the liberal denomination whose members vetted their own ministers. In theory, the Unitarian religion was considered the best of two worlds, because it accepted the lessons of reason while acknowledging the religious traditions of Boston's Congregational heritage. Progressive Unitarians believed that God is in every person and the individual is a source of moral light, at his/her best when self-reliant.

The religious group included many prominent merchants who heard Sunday sermons given by liberal reformers. William Ellery Channing, the Federal Street Church minister, warned his congregation that "the prosperous and the distinguished of this world...are among the last to comprehend the worth of a human being, to penetrate into the evils of society, or to impact to it a fresh impulse." Boston elites, he believed, favored the status quo. Therefore, he sought out upper middle-class audiences, urging them to be involved in abolition.

In a similar manner, Unitarian minister Theodore Parker went on the lecture circuit. He exposed the underside of contemporary social relations, shattering the moral authority of the ruling elite.

He concluded: "Boston is a now shop, with the aim of a shop, and the morals of a shop, and the politics of a shop."

The Brattle Street Congregation

John's home church had a long and distinguished history in Boston. The Brattle Street Congregation began in 1699 on Brattle Square, named for merchant Thomas Brattle. After many name changes, from Scollay Square to the current day Government Center, the historically bustling area continues its vibrancy and is now the site of Boston's City Hall.

The church was referred to as the "The Manifesto Church" since it originated with liberal declarations that refuted pre-election of souls and favored democratically electing its clergy. Boston's John Hancock was the chairman of the church building committee, and he donated a thousand pounds and a bell to the church where John Adams and his son John Quincy Adams were parishioners. In Simmons' time, Edward Everett (later a senator) was a minister, followed by John G. Palfrey from 1818-31. Palfrey was a Conscience Whig who freed the sixteen slaves he inherited from his father, a Louisiana plantation owner. After serving as a professor of Biblical Literature at Harvard Divinity School, Palfrey became a state representative and then a United States congressman. For Unitarians, religion and social responsibility were synonymous, and as a churchgoer, Simmons mixed with his fellow parishioners and ministers and surely talked about the issues of slavery. How much these conversations influenced him is undocumented, but they certainly must have engaged him.

Until 1833, Massachusetts churches were supported by state funds. After that date churches had to compete for parishioners in order to pay operating expenses. Pews were sold to subsidize the no longer publically funded congregations. More acceptable practices and creeds were introduced, wooing a more discerning religious audience.

John's Minister

Samuel K. Lothrop ministered to John's Unitarian parish after 1834. On John's forty-sixth birthday, October 30, 1842, Lothrop gave a sermon about "A Good Man," one whose qualities included being an independent decision maker with energy of character. "Salvation by character" was the ideal practice proposed in Unitarian circles. One's good deeds took precedence over pre-election to God's grace. Unitarianism was an optimistic religion that stressed self-improvement, a fine fit with Boston's own self-image—tailored to John's approach to life.

Lothrop lived in the parsonage at 42 Court Street, which had been donated by John Hancock's Aunt Lydia. Samuel Lothrop was a relatively conservative Unitarian. He believed that Christ was the son of God, not just a prophet as more progressive Unitarians were asserting. Lothrop wrote: "I am decidedly a liberal Congregationalist." However, Lothrop's actions suggest his more conservative side. In a collection of his writings edited by his son, Thornton Kirkland

Lothrup, the senior Lothrop tells the story of meeting a former Harvard classmate in London. The man was a Southerner who wouldn't change his earlier dinner plans to suit his companions. Lothrop faulted the man's manners but said nothing at that time about the issue of southern slavery. This omission in Lothrop's anecdote leaves one wondering what the minister thought of his dinner partner's politics.

Enter Miss Dix

Perhaps the most influential Unitarian activist for John was not one of these male ministers, but a female Federal Street Church congregant, Dorothea Lynde Dix. Like Quaker women, Unitarian women were empowered by their religious training to favor and advocate for individual conscience above institutional rules. Dorothea was an intellectually gifted child who yearned for personal growth despite periods of loneliness, isolation and hardship.

At age twelve, she ran away from her Methodist minister father and lived with her wealthy grandmother in Boston. She felt emotionally orphaned saying, "I wander alone with no one to guide me." At nineteen, she opened a free evening school for poor children in Boston, where she was known as a strict and demanding teacher. In 1836, she traveled to Liverpool, England. Accounts vary as to whether Dorothea was ill with a severe respiratory illness or depression, which was then called melancholia. But she was well cared for by fellow Unitarians, her hosts, the Rathbones. Through them, Dorothea learned about prison reform. Back in Boston on March 28, 1841, she was asked by Harvard Divinity School student John Nichols to teach Sunday school at an East Cambridge jail. Harsh prison conditions at the Middlesex County House of Correction shocked Dix. She abhorred seeing the mentally ill incarcerated with criminals and alcoholics. She secured a court order to make physical improvements at the jail, including hearth fires to warm the freezing inmates.

This experience was the first in her lifelong work on behalf of public health. She gained her victories as a single woman with no voting rights, unable to hold any political office, barred from speaking in public. As a woman, Dix was not allowed to deliver sermons, attend college or enter the professions, making her achievements all the more outstanding. Never marrying, Dix traveled constantly, but had no permanent address insisting "the world is my home." She visited jails and almshouses around New England, demanding full access. An early self-taught social worker, Dix collected data and wrote careful reports on public abuses of the mentally ill.

Dix was concerned that many female inmates in the jails she visited had worked in the Lowell mills. She believed industrial labor harmed women's bodies. Unlike mill proponents who stressed the economic power and independence such work provided, Dorothea believed women were morally superior to men and that their good deeds should be done without any regard for self-profit. Although her advancement of care for the mentally ill was quite liberal, her opinion of women's responsibilities to be nurturing wives and mothers was decidedly conservative. She never supported women's rights groups or the abolition cause.

But when it came to the care of the mentally ill, Dix was a tireless fighter. To avoid the controversy of any woman speaking in front of a mixed audience, Dix collaborated with Dr. Samuel Gridley Howe, Director of the Perkins School for the Blind. Since Dix could not take legislative action herself, Howe became Dix's public voice. He successfully petitioned the Massachusetts legislature for funds to expand the State Mental Hospital in Worcester in 1843. Dix originally lobbied for a new hospital, but settled for a 150-bed addition to this central Massachusetts site.

The Political is Personal

Dix traveled around New England promoting her plans for improved mental health facilities. In 1843 she met and lobbied Cyrus Butler, a wealthy donor from Providence, Rhode Island; he promised Dix a $40,000 donation for a mental health hospital if she could obtain matching funds. In 1844, Dix went on a tour of Rhode Island to solicit such donors, and she visited John Simmons' hometown. In an era without effective medicine or therapeutic care, the mentally ill were often placed in state custody and housed in local jails. In a cell in Little Compton, Dix observed John's cousin Abram Simmons (son of William and Rebecca Simmons) isolated in an unheated six by eight foot space without light and fresh air. After examining Abram, Dix wrote a newspaper article, which was published in the April 10th *Providence Journal* chronicling her observations. Dix described Abram Simmons, as living "in utter darkness," crying, "Poor Tom's a-cold." According to Thomas Brown's biography *Dorothea Dix: New England Reformer*, Dix met with state legislators to obtain Abram's release from town custody. However, Abram died before the matter was settled. Dix was livid. In correspondence with George B. Emerson on May 11, 1844, Dix accused the townspeople of "murder in the second degree." No record has been found of John's position on the matter. It's fair to assume that the loss of Abram Simmons only deepened John's family sorrows.

Dix continued to work tirelessly to secure therapeutic and comfortable settings for the curable and incurable alike. For the next ten years Dorothea went on fact-finding missions to many states both north and south, persuading state legislatures to establish hospitals. Encouraged by her successes, Dix eventually lobbied on behalf of a proposed federal land grant of ten million acres, whose sale would fund public asylums for the benefit of blind, deaf, mute and insane persons. While her plan secured passage from both the United States Senate and House of Representatives, in 1854 President Franklin Pierce vetoed the bill stating that such institutions were not the government's responsibility. The *Richmond Enquirer* mocked the bill, which would have established asylums in every state, as "originating in the crochet of a crazy old woman." Defeated, a discouraged Dix retreated to Europe, where she took up similar reforms.

Private Sorrow

Despite personal financial prosperity, John was no stranger to the inequities of life. Immigrants lacked economic freedom, slaves had no personal or political freedom, women lacked political, legal and educational freedom, and the ill lacked proper care. His religion encouraged social reforms with these answers: abolition, education, economic justice and compassionate care.

In addition to the lack of fairness in his mid-century society, John's family heartaches begged the question "Is it fair?" In the span of two years three of his grandchildren died. On February 15, 1853, Theodore's daughter Ella, age one and a half, succumbed to scarlet fever, an infectious bacterial disease that commonly affected children in a pre-antibiotics era. The following year, on August twentieth, Theodore's third daughter, Lily, also passed away. To have three sons and now two granddaughters die before him was an enormous sorrow. Imagine his feelings when ten days after burying Lily, his only grandson, John III, died at nine years of age. John's grief, along with Ann's and the rest of the family's, surely altered his view of the future. Bereft, this successful head of the family would seek to remedy his pain.

Older Ann Small Simmons

In this family album photo owned by Little Compton Historical Society, Ann Small Simmons, in her fifties, appears to be an attractive and fashionably dressed woman in this pre-Civil War photograph.

Older John Simmons

Despite suffering from Bright's Disease, an older white-haired John stood tall for this photograph found in a family album in Little Compton Historical Society's archival collection.

1, 2 and 3 Arlington Street, Boston, Massachusetts

Three grand French academic style mansions facing the Boston Public Garden at 1, 2 and 3 Arlington Street in Boston were custom built in 1861 for John Simmons, yet they did not entice Ann, Mary Ann, or Alvina to make the move across town.

Photo courtesy of Denise Doherty Pappas.

CHAPTER SEVEN: HALF OF MY LIFE IS GONE

Life's tragedy is that we get old too soon and wise too late.
~Benjamin Franklin

In His 50s

No stranger to the graveyard, John was powerless when three more relatives died between 1855 and 1857. Along with his elderly mother, Nancy, John's granddaughter Daisy died in 1855. The following year Theodore's fifth daughter was born to much delight. However, Genevieve (like three sisters before her) was dead within five months. While Theodore and Harriet had five daughters in the first five years of their marriage, only their second daughter, Harriet, survived. Along with her cousin Anna White Simmons, Harriet was famous for bringing a smile to the face of her otherwise very serious grandfather.

By 1857, despite his personal grief, as a shrewd man of business, John remained on the lookout for profitable investment opportunities. That August, a ship carrying a significant supply of gold from San Francisco to the eastern banks of New England sank in a hurricane, precipitating a financial collapse, known as the Panic of 1857. A two-year depression followed. Midwest grain prices and land values began dropping with the decline in demand for agriculture after Europe's recovery from the Crimean War. This resulted in bank, railroad, construction, and factory failures, principally in the Northeast. Free-labor industry suffered the most. Since world demand for raw cotton remained stable, Southerners were less affected by the economic downslide. Cotton kings felt vindicated, since their slave labor system remained profitable.

Responding to a drop in the real estate market precipitated by the depression, John expanded his fortune by diversifying into Boston real estate. John acquired a portfolio of commercial properties in downtown Boston and in other emerging areas of his city. According to historian Kenneth L. Mark, John carefully bought buildings on Franklin and Arch streets, Franklin and Hawley streets, Milk and Devonshire streets, Water Street, Columbus Avenue, Commercial Street, and Isabella and Ferdinand streets in Boston. He continued to increase his real estate holdings, improving the properties and collecting substantial rents.

Yankee Power

While John Simmons was a leader in commercial real estate ownership, Boston was the leading literary center of the nation. The cultural hub was home to numerous authors and was the publishing center of the country. James Russell Lowell and Henry Wadsworth Longfellow started *The Atlantic Monthly*, a popular journal published in Boston, and Oliver Wendell Holmes, a Dean at Harvard Medical School, was the titular godfather of the magazine. Holmes wrote a series of essays called "The Autocrat of the Breakfast Table," literary articles full of self-deprecating anecdotes that men of John Simmons' age and class enjoyed. Set at a boarding house breakfast table, these pieces recorded fictional conversations between various boarders that reflected the anxiety of uncertain contemporary times. Fathers were no longer the unquestioned authority figures in families, according to Holmes' fictional account.

Holmes realized he could not be a despot, a ruler with unlimited power and authority—certainly not on this earth. The limitations of wealth and power must also have been all too apparent to sixty-year-old John, who no doubt felt powerless in the face of his grandchildren's premature deaths. "The Old Man Dreams," a poem by Holmes, is narrated by a seasoned older man. Could John have had similar wishes?

> O for one hour of youthful joy!
>   Give back my twentieth Spring!
> I'd rather laugh a bright-haired boy
>   Than reign a gray-beard king!
>
> Off with the wrinkled spoils of age!
> Away with learning's crown!
> Tear out life's wisdom-written page,
> And dash its trophies down!

However, by the end of the poem, the narrator tells his better Angel he would miss his wife and children too much if he returned to his youth. He decides to stay and act his age, appreciating the family he has made.

117

Losing Theodore

Although literature may enlighten, tragedy is the cruelest teacher of all. In July of 1857, Theodore, age twenty-eight, applied for a US passport. He intended to travel with his wife and only surviving child; like his brother John, Theodore may have been seeking a healthier climate. Yet on May 13, 1858, John received the most crushing news a parent will ever hear: his only surviving son, Theodore Augustus, was dead of consumption at twenty-nine. Theodore left behind his widow and his daughter, another Harriet, age five. Losing his last male heir, who would have carried on the legacy of his clothing empire, was a deeply felt personal and professional tragedy for sixty-two-year-old John and his wife of nearly forty years. In that same year, Ann Small Simmons became paralyzed, presumably from a stroke. Thus, forty years after starting his own business and as one of the most successful clothing manufacturers in the country, Simmons retired from the trade.

Real Estate Investments

John continued buying property, with a special plan in mind. In a sense, real estate acquisition and management was a continuation of the journey John took from Little Compton to Boston as a young man. John's strong business sense coupled with his energy and work ethic channeled personal sorrow into action. His Arlington Street construction plan was his loving attempt to bring some happiness back into the lives of his wife and daughters—joy that Theodore's death had taken away.

In 1860, John bought land at 1, 2 and 3 Arlington Street across from the Public Garden, and he commissioned well-respected architects and designers Gridley J. F. Bryant and Arthur Gilman to design three grand French academic style mansions. This style was considered the height of sophistication in pre-Civil War Boston. Bryant and Gilman's earlier works included the Arlington Street Church and the Charles Street Jail. Simmons' three residences were joined together to give the appearance of being a single building, and his plan was to move his entire family into this up-and-coming section of town. One house would be for Ann, one for Mary Ann, and one for Alvina. How disappointed John must have felt when his wife and his daughters all refused to move, believing Arlington Street (directly across the Common and the Public Garden) was too far out of town. As a result, in 1862 John sold the property to William F. Weld, whose great-great-grandson, also named William F. Weld, was the Governor of the Commonwealth of Massachusetts from 1991 to 1997.

Henry Wadsworth Longfellow

In the middle of the nineteenth century, poets were popular chroniclers of current events. Henry Wadsworth Longfellow, the internationally beloved poet from Cambridge, was a distant relative of John's; both men were descendants of Pricilla and John Alden. Longfellow's life history mirrored his distant cousin John's; both men had daughters they treasured. Longfellow's poem "The Children's Hour" echoed John's protective stance toward Mary Ann and Alvina.

> I have you fast in my fortress
> And will not let you depart,
> But put you down into the dungeon
> In the round-tower of my heart.
>
> And there I will keep you forever,
> Yes, forever and a day,
> Till the walls shall crumble to ruin,
> And moulder in dust away!

Longfellow, ten year's John's junior, had lost his first wife as a young man. A Dante scholar, Longfellow brilliantly articulated the sorrows that John experienced through the early deaths of his family members. "Mezzo Cammin" artfully describes the regret, fear and sadness after suffering great loss. Like his cousin John, the poet held back on certain emotional topics and considered this poem too personal to publish during his lifetime.

> Half of my life is gone, and I have let
>   The years slip from me and have not fulfilled
>   The aspiration of my youth, to build
>   Some tower of song with lofty parapet.
> Not indolence, nor pleasure, nor the fret
>   Of restless passions that would not be stilled,
>   But sorrow, and a care that almost killed,
>   Kept me from what I may accomplish yet;
> Though, half-way up the hill, I see the Past

Lying beneath me with its sounds and sights,—
A city in the twilight dim and vast,
With smoking roofs, soft bells, and gleaming lights,—
And hear above me on the autumnal blast
The cataract of Death far thundering from the heights.

Despite his own difficulties, and in response to his personal losses, John developed a plan that would achieve radical results. He placed his faith in real estate, confident in its ability to provide steady profits. Earlier in his career, John lost money in stock speculation, but he trusted commercial real estate as a more secure way to remain profitable and ensure his financial holdings would not depreciate.

Age of Anxiety

By 1859, however, with the country on the brink of civil war, security in any business area was threatened. The South felt betrayed by Northerners agitating for slave uprisings; the North felt betrayed by Southern politicians trying to legalize slavery in new territories. Each side was angry with the other for disturbing the status quo. On December 8, 1859, five days after abolitionist John Brown was hanged, relations between the North and South were at their lowest point ever.

Cotton Whigs held a meeting in Faneuil Hall. John Simmons and his friend, textile merchant Joseph Sawyer, attended this eleventh-hour meeting. Attendants at the "union meeting" described by the *Boston Courier Report* felt that a compromise permitting the status quo would be preferable to secession. As war seemed inevitable, cotton sales plummeted and manufacturing jobs were already being lost. Amos A. Lawrence, representing the feelings of his fellow conservative textile merchants asked defensively: "Shall we uphold the union or break it up?"

These men were thinking of their balance sheets, but they also wanted to prevent bloodshed. Edward Everett and Amos A. Lawrence traveled to Washington to push for the Crittenden Resolution, a last legislative stab at preventing disunion, believing it might prevent war. Northerners, desperate for a compromise, made huge concessions to a secession-threatening South, all to no avail.

Two years earlier, Abraham Lincoln had proclaimed "A house divided cannot stand." But with war imminent in 1860, and when pressed about his stand on slavery, president-elect Lincoln was non-committal, and tersely reasserted his oath of office: "I'll defend the Constitution." Yankee appeasement reasoned thus: since the union had always been held together with a patchwork of compromises, why not have one last try?

Matthew Vassar's Example

In January of 1861, a few months before the start of the Civil War, John and Ann Simmons heard about of the incorporation of Vassar College. Matthew Vassar, an English immigrant, had become the largest beer brewer in the United States, and he donated $408,000 to found a college for women in Poughkeepsie, New York. Why did he do this? Vassar was a childless benefactor, but his step-niece, Lydia Booth, ran a female seminary in the 1840s. Lydia's work impressed Vassar and convinced him that providing higher education for women was not only noble, it was feasible. At the same time, however, Vassar's nephews were lobbying him for a major endowment to a hospital. Unfortunately, Lydia Booth died in 1854 before her uncle made his decision, leaving both the seminary and the hospital in limbo. But Booth's successor at her Cottage Hill Seminary, Professor Milo P. Jewett, joined Vassar's church and persuaded the millionaire to endow a women's college. In 1864 Vassar gave a speech crediting Lydia for awakening him to the need for such an institution. For this reason, Lydia Booth was recognized as "the real founder of Vassar College."

In 1861, Mary Lyon's Seminary in Holyoke changed from a three- to a four-year course, but to call this center of learning a college for women was still too inflammatory. It wasn't until 1893 that the seminary curriculum was phased out, and the name Mary Lyons' Seminary was changed to Mt. Holyoke College. Smith College and Wellesley College would not be founded until 1875, three years after Boston University began admitting women to all its divisions, making it the first coeducational college in New England. Times were changing.

Enormous Loss

The idea of women as intellectually worthy as men was a radical concept in the 1860s. While John Simmons' portfolio equaled Matthew Vassar's, John had something Vassar did not—a family of women, including two daughters and two granddaughters. No doubt John's wife of forty-three years had desires and dreams for her offspring. Like her husband, Ann witnessed enormous societal, cultural and personal changes during her sixty-three years. But by May of 1861, Ann Small Simmons was dead. She had never recovered after three final years of paralysis. Anything she may have had to say about the future of women could only be enacted by John.

Anna Simmons White Rowe as a young girl

Anna followed her family's tradition of being impeccably well-dressed.

Photo courtesy of Little Compton Historical Society.

Alvina White

Alvina White, born in 1857, is described as the "adopted daughter of E.A. White"
in the Simmons Family Album. This younger Alvina's true identity and life story
remain a mystery.

Photo courtesy of Little Compton Historical Society.

CHAPTER EIGHT: THY WILL BE DONE

An investment in knowledge always pays the best interest.
~Benjamin Franklin

John Carries On

Mary Bailey, Ann's cousin from Cape Cod, stayed at Tremont Street as John's housekeeper after Ann passed away. On Sunday mornings, she cooked John his favorite "johnnycakes," which he shared with his granddaughter Anna. After breakfast, the two would attend the Brattle Street Church. On Sunday afternoons, John visited friends from his manufacturing days. Starting out at Tremont Street, wearing a long black coat and huge black cravat, the cane-carrying gentleman in his sixties visited his confidant and business acquaintance Joseph Sawyer at his home at 31 Commonwealth Avenue, now the fashionable end of town.

Although Joseph Sawyer was a generation younger than John the two shared a similar history. Sawyer hailed from Massachusetts Bay Colony ancestors. At fourteen he began work as a clerk in a retail dry goods store on Hanover Street, so impressing his boss, Joshua Stetson, with his reliability and steady work ethic he was promoted to the role of jobber (the agent between textile manufacturers and retail store owners.) No doubt John and Sawyer crossed paths in their work. Sawyer eventually became the largest company shareholder in his role as the president of many New England textile mills—a tribute to the way in which he worked his way up in the woolen importing business. His 1901 obituary would reveal Sawyer had given over half a million dollars to various charities during his career. Presumably John and Sawyer worked together enough so that the two men developed a personal relationship in addition to their professional one. During John's later excursions to Sawyer's home, the two friends may have discussed the wartime business efforts of Alvin Rose, Simmons' business partner in the 1840s. Rose became one of the leading Civil War contractors supplying clothing, tents and blankets worth $8,700,000 dollars to the United States military—a substantial amount of money for the times.

The devastating effects of the Civil War reaffirmed John's understanding of life's unfairness. At all levels of society, families were struck by emotional and financial losses. As a widower, John suffered the absence of his beloved wife Ann, and perhaps his personal pain deepened his sensitivity to the financial hardship women experienced when they were single, abandoned, or widowed, or when their husbands experienced business failures. According to Kenneth L. Mark in *Delayed by Fire*, when speaking to his trusted friend Sawyer, John shared this assessment: it was critical that women be given training needed for self-maintenance, a conclusion drawn from the overwhelming number of post-war women forced to be sole providers.

Dix Returns

After returning from Europe, Dorothea Dix put her leadership skills to good use. Thanks to her prior experience with medical doctors and institutions she found herself once again at the forefront of American relief and reform efforts. During the Civil War, she served as Superintendent of the United States Army Nurses. Dix hired her own nurses, provided training, and organized field hospitals. With a career history of exposing errors and demanding corrections, Dix was never one to compromise. She often criticized doctors for their drinking habits and their unhygienic medical practices. While she was a hero to the wounded, many on her staff and her superiors disliked her rigid medical-administrative rules. Since women were then new to the nursing profession, she wanted them to be above reproach. She required her nurses to be plain looking and over thirty years of age. Nurses were forbidden to wear decorative clothing and they had nine o'clock curfews. Dix feared her nurses fraternizing with male patients. Louisa May Alcott, who served as a nurse at the Union Hotel Hospital in December of 1862, described Dix as "a kind old soul, but very queer, fussy and arbitrary; no one likes her and I don't wonder."

Never one to seek popular public favor, Dix had nonetheless hoped to be seen as the Florence Nightingale of the Civil War. But that honor went instead to Clara Barton, a freelance nurse a generation younger than Dix who helped families with missing soldiers. Dix's plainspoken manner offended some who did not want to hear truth as she saw it; however, with her strict standards, Dix professionalized the nursing field and allowed women to integrate Civil War health care. Until then it was a male dominated field, and Dix was the first woman with executive level governmental authority in American history. Three thousand Northern women served as paid Union Army nurses in wartime. The Dix nurses proved themselves strong, courageous and capable, seeding the way for future employment reforms for women.

Return to Little Compton

Both before and after Ann's death, John spent significant time in his hometown of Little Compton, Rhode Island. His brother, Valentine, and his sisters, Mary, Comfort, and Lydia, still lived there with their families. Every summer, John took the train to Tiverton, Rhode Island. At the station, John's manservant Collins met him with his horse and carriage. Together they rode the sixteen miles to the four-room home in which Simmons had lived in as a boy. John turned to his youthful summertime pleasures: hunting and fishing. He even ordered an elaborately carved chair with the heads of hunting dogs and guns to be custom-made for his Boston mansion—a reminder of his favorite rural activities.

In that relaxed family atmosphere on the peninsula, John no doubt assessed his legacy. He had time to reflect on his financial success—he'd left Little Compton with five dollars in his pocket almost a half-century earlier. An astute businessman, John knew how other wealthy men allocated their assets. Whether fortunes were amassed through hard work or inheritance, John might have surmised, along with other wealthy men of his generation, it would be easy to weaken the work ethic of his heirs by leaving them too large an inheritance. To counteract potential trouble, a renowned member of The Boston Associates, Jonathan Jackson, made a trust in his will providing for his daughters but excluding their husbands. Doubtless, John did not want his nemesis George Ditson, Mary Ann's first husband, to get a penny from the Simmons estate. As a long-time resident of Boston, John had observed wealthy men endowing Harvard College, Massachusetts General Hospital, The Boston Athenaeum, and the Lowell Institute (a lecture series sponsored in John Lowell's honor). At the same time, Boston society discussed, debated and defended the optimistic legacy of transcendentalism, with its faith in the perfectibility of people, its disregard for dogma and its impulse to champion the oppressed.

Yankee Philanthropy

John lived and worked in a city with a large number of upper class Bostonians descended from the Puritans, replete with a tradition of public service. These elites were schooled with a sense of moral stewardship, secure that they knew the best practices not only for the City on the Hill, but beyond. As art patrons, Boston's elites dictated perceptions regarding culture, and their reach extended to hospitals, universities, museums and libraries, which became part of their legacy. While proper Bostonians would not always hold the reigns of political power—especially as the population grew—as philanthropists they held enormous institutional and cultural control over society. Through their financial donations and board memberships, elites managed to shape Boston as a cultural and business hub, and lay the foundations for its future.

John Simmons' Will

While John was not a Boston Brahmin, he had a comparable fortune. A Macon, Georgia newspaper article on June 18, 1866 told the nation that John Simmons was one of the ten richest men in Boston. Most importantly, he possessed a deeply felt desire to make the most prudent and worthwhile use of his increasingly valuable real estate fortune. For this reason, on June 1, 1867, he signed a meticulously crafted thirty-three page will at the law office of his friend, Benjamin Brooks.

John decided his daughters, Mary Ann and Alvina, and his granddaughters, Anna and Harriet, would each receive a substantial legacy, but not immense wealth. They would inherit enough money to be comfortable, but not rich like John Simmons, and in his will he referred to his daughters and granddaughters as "beloved." They would each receive five-thousand dollars a year for the rest of their lives. John gave his remaining siblings a thousand dollars each. Mary Bailey, Ann's niece and John's housekeeper, received a lifetime yearly income of four-hundred dollars. Since John shared the contents of his will with only a few close associates, his relatives may have been surprised by his major asset allocation—founding

Simmons Female College, the original name for the school—which may have been revealed to them only after his death.

Most strikingly, future Simmons College Trustee Henry S. Rowe reported in "The Ancestry of John Simmons: Founder of Simmons College" that John wanted his college to be a tuition-free institution. Why tuition free? As a businessman, Simmons understood his intended customers, in this case, working and middle class young women. He realized he needed to minimize the opportunity costs these women faced by foregoing income while attending college. Yet Simmons also knew there was no market demand for college-educated women in 1867. So how to entice attendance?

John took note not only of Matthew Vassar's efforts regarding women's education, but of Congressional action regarding financial matters. In 1862 the U.S. government set an important precedent by enacting the Morrill Act. With state appropriations covering costs, this act provided tuition free education for agricultural and mechanical training to land grant colleges. Their curriculum provided training in the areas of great need such as engineering and agricultural business, and greatly reduced costs enabled many worthy students to attend college. John Simmons knew tuition freedom would enable more women to attend and train for the skilled jobs of the future.

To fill and maintain his scholarship coffers, John requested that once the rental income from selected real estate properties reached $500,000, the college could be incorporated. Future operating funds for Simmons Female College would also come from the rental profits on properties held in trust. John had carefully won his fortune by thrift and he was determined to have his fortune spent in helping others when he was gone.

So from 1867 on, John monitored his investments, and informed his lawyer of his philanthropic intention. On January 15, 1870, John returned to Brooks' office and signed a fifteen-page codicil to his will, which updated his carefully managed endowment funds. Wisely, John Simmons appointed Joseph Sawyer, Benjamin Brooks and his son-in-law Edward White as trustees of the estate.

Other Textile Trade Philanthropists

In 1849, textile mill owner Amos A. Lawrence donated ten thousand dollars to found Lawrence College (now Lawrence University) in Appleton, Wisconsin, a town named for his father-in-law. In later years, following John's lead, other clothing manufacturers also gave generously to fund educational institutions. In 1882, Paul Tulane, a New York clothing manufacturer with a prosperous store in New Orleans, gave two million dollars to endow Tulane University. Likewise, another wealthy manufacturer, Augustus Julliard, posthumously donated a fortune to the New York Institute of Musical Art, which was then renamed in his honor. In pre-income tax times, there were no monetary incentives to make charitable donations. So why did so many business leaders donate to college education? Some believed in education itself, some sought a life memorial, and some favored special groups like women.

Bright's Disease

As he aged, John suffered from "Bright's Disease," a kidney malfunction named for English physician Dr. Richard Bright who first described it in 1827. "Bright's Disease" is a historical term describing a range of kidney ailments. Nephritis is frequently accompanied by severe back pain, fever, and edema. Symptoms of this disease include kidney stones, infection and hypertension. There was no cure available during Simmons' lifetime. John may have been treated with blood cupping, warm baths and diuretics to relieve his edema.

Bright's Disease was the cause of John Simmons' death on August 29, 1870 in Little Compton, Rhode Island. As per custom, the seventy-three-year-old benefactor was waked the next day at his mansion on Tremont Street in Boston. He was buried at Mount Auburn Cemetery in Cambridge in the family plot he had the foresight to purchase thirty-three years earlier. In this exquisite resting place of major nineteenth century leaders, John was buried next to his wife Ann, his sons, and four granddaughters and one grandnephew.

Posthumous Appraisals

After his death, John Simmons received the praise and appreciation he had modestly shunned during his lifetime. On September 10, 1870, *The Boston Advertiser* said this of John:

> Mr. Simmons was a man of close business habits, and applied himself to the management of

135

his affairs with great persistency. He was genial in nature and fond of social intercourse but he seldom confided his plans to others. He was naturally a very kind-hearted man and he performed many acts of charity which were known to few. Unostentatious in all things, he never sought or held public office, though he was once a captain of a militia company, and for a time was known as Captain Simmons. He was always straightforward and scrupulously just in his transactions, and when he made a friend, the friendship was a lasting one.

The press gave glowing accounts of this pioneering dealer in ready-made clothing. His endowment would establish the first college in the United States to combine liberal arts and professional studies for women. The September 11, 1870 issue of *The College Courant*, published by Yale University, included this summary of John's radical plan:

He had occasion to employ great numbers of working women and he early became acquainted with the needs of this class, which has grown to be very numerous in the vicinity. He found that they were incapacitated for their labor by their lack of training. He was constantly beset with applications for work from those who were unable to sew a single seam properly, and he saw much of the suffering of the class of destitute needlewomen which it became the object of his life to mitigate. He was at once convinced of the uselessness of charity in relieving them from the difficulties and evil which oppressed them. He saw that it was industrial education that they needed and determined to devote his fortune to the foundation of an institution for the purpose which should supply young and indigent girls with practical training in some of the pursuits of art, science, or industry by which they might be enabled to get a living. And for this purpose he planned and toiled constantly during the last ten years of his life. Always frugal in his habits and style of living, he continued to practice self-denial and self-sacrifice in the later years of his life, when his rapidly accumulating fortune and the fashions of the day would have warranted a freer personal expenditure. Yet he never was penurious and never ceased to enjoy the pleasures of rural life in his country home in Little Compton.

At this time, only one percent of potential college age students actually attended college, and not everyone looked favorably on John Simmons' idea. On September 22, 1870, *The Nation* reported "his charitable feeling toward them [women] doubtless prompted him to devise the remedy which has just been revealed to the public. It will be tried most appropriately in a state notorious for having a surplus of women."

John Simmons' plan was a novel, progressive arrangement for this marginalized, underserved population. But once again, an unforeseen event would alter John's unique and remarkable intention.

The Great Boston Fire

*While dwarfed in national memory by the Great Chicago Fire of 1871, the Great
Boston Fire of November 1872 was equally devastating to those affected, particularly the women scholars who were to benefit by John Simmons' college endowment.*
Photo courtesy of the Trustees of the Boston Public Library.

Dorothea Lynde Dix

Unitarian Dorothea Lynde Dix (1802-1887) was a self-taught social worker who professionalized nursing for women and made a generous donation to John Simmons' plan for the founding of the College.

Photo courtesy of The Boston Athenaeum.

Lydia Grinnell

Lydia Grinnell, from New Bedford, Massachusetts, was the first African American to graduate from Simmons College in 1915. She later attended Harvard Graduate School of Education. She died in Washington, DC in 1946.

Photo courtesy of Simmons College Archives.

Simmons College, Class of 1906

These happy graduates from the Class of 1906 would eventually be joined by 60,000 sister alums and four thousand brother alums from the graduate schools of Simmons College.

Photo courtesy of Simmons College Archives.

CHAPTER NINE: WHEEL OF FORTUNE

The doors of wisdom are never shut.
    ~Benjamin Franklin

A Turn of the Wheel

By 1872, Simmons had been dead for two years, but his wheel of fortune continued to spin. Curiously, his legacy came to be tied to that of another John, a leader he never met. John Stanhope Damrell was the forty-four-year-old Chief of the four-hundred and seventy man Boston Fire Department. Chief Damrell came from a fire-fighting family, and in 1872 Massachusetts officials sent the firefighter to Chicago to learn the best fire prevention practices after that city's disaster in 1871. The Great Chicago Fire had killed three-hundred people, left one-hundred thousand homeless, and destroyed seventeen thousand buildings the first night of the fire. The raging blaze caused two-hundred million dollars in property damage. Following a dry summer, the legendary fire sparked at 13 Dekover Street in a barn owned by Patrick and Catherine O'Leary. Mrs. O'Leary claimed to have been in bed along with her five children when the fire began around nine o'clock on the night of October 8, 1871. She believed a neighbor had trespassed and entered her barn to steal milk—and one cow being milked kicked over a kerosene lamp. From an inventory of six cows, one horse and wagon and harness, only one calf survived the inferno, which spread quickly in thirty-mile-per-hour winds. Fortunately, a rainstorm the next day helped to put out the fire.

Chief Damrell returned to Boston from his fact-finding mission with a list of critically needed fire equipment. He requested a steam engine for the most vulnerable area: downtown—the clothing merchandise district, which held warehouses, dry goods stores, counting houses, stables, and leather factories. Damrell knew that clothing remaining in inventory was not taxed, so many merchants had stuffed their attics with these highly flammable goods. Unfortunately, his request for a steam engine was turned down, the rationale being that it was too expensive. Next, Damrell appealed to the water board for new pipes but again he was disappointed. Author Peter Canellos summarized: "Yankee parsimoniousness undermined Yankee preparedness."

In addition, Boston's firefighting efforts on behalf of over a quarter million residents were severely undermined in the fall of that year when Boston's horse community was devastated by distemper. Firefighting horses were too sick to work. By Saturday, October 26th, unable to replace their downed animals, firefighters strapped themselves in front of fire engines and dragged their equipment where it was needed. To ensure Boston's safety, five-hundred extra men were put "on call" for emergencies. They were to be paid $1 for showing up and 25 cents for each hour of fighting fires.

The Great Boston Fire

According to Stephanie Schorow, author of *Boston on Fire: A History of Fires and Firefighting in Boston*, at seven o'clock on the evening of Saturday, November 9, 1872, a fire of unknown origin blazed up in a building on the corner of Kingston and Summer Streets. In the five-story building filled with flammable material, the fire burst in to the elevator shaft. That night two alarms sounded at 7:24 and 7:29, but by the time firefighters arrived at 7:45 it was too late to save the building. The fire hoses were only long enough to reach four-story buildings, so water failed to reach the fifth-floor mansard building roofs. Their attics had been packed with inventory, and as a result, the fire spread from rooftop to rooftop, escalating out of control.

In desperation, Postmaster General William Burt got permission from Damrell to use gunpowder to blow up some buildings, creating an artificial barrier in an attempt to stop the fire's spread. Unfortunately, the natural gas running through the Boston buildings could only be shut off building by building, so the natural gas combined with explosives further fueled the fire. Observing from his home on Beacon Hill, Dr. Oliver Wendell Holmes said, "I saw the fire eating its way straight toward my deposits." The fire raged through Franklin, Congress and Federal Streets, but thanks to a steam engine sent by rail from Portsmouth, New Hampshire, the Old South Meeting House was saved from destruction. The fire was stopped at Washington Street and was officially extinguished by the morning of Monday, November 11th.

Eight million pounds of wool had gone up in smoke. Ten million dollars of consigned goods were lost. One thousand firms were burned out in seven-hundred and seventy-six buildings on sixty acres, and seventy-six million dollars in damages were reported. Ten firefighters lost their lives at the scene, and two others died shortly thereafter. Twenty-thousand people were jobless, and countless thousands were left homeless. In response to the disaster, approximately eighty-thousand dollars were raised for a firefighter's fund.

Schorow reports Minister Henry Ward Beecher (the brother of Catharine Beecher and Harriet Beecher Stowe) pragmatically suggested, "Instead of asking if God meant to humble Boston, let us look to the future and see what are the lessons to be learned from such a conflagration as this." Blame and responsibility for the disaster fell to the sick horses, the fifth-floor mansard roofs, ineffective water mains, and volunteers' hoses, which didn't connect with those of the Boston Fire Department. In spite of the disastrous extent of the devastation, Boston's fire was mostly forgotten by future generations, while Chicago's fire remained legendary.

But the Great Boston Fire prompted the adoption of corrective firefighting measures in the Bay State. In response to the Great Boston Fire, difficult to locate and identify fire hydrants were painted red, and fire alarm updates were implemented. Before the fire, a policeman had to be found and alerted to open the fire alarm box. After the fire, keyless entry to fire alarm boxes was made available to all. In addition, universal valve sizes were created and installed on hydrants so that outside fire departments and local volunteers were able to connect hoses and valves, ensuring a steady flow of water to extinguish fires.

Reversal of Fortune

In 1872 John Simmons' estate was still in probate. Most of the properties designated as a revenue stream for his proposed college were located in Boston's fire-ravaged district. They, too, had burned to the ground. To compound matters, twenty of the thirty-three insurance companies went bankrupt trying to cover losses, and the real estate that John Simmons had carefully selected, maintained, and guarded to provide income for Simmons Female College (now known as Simmons College) was not covered. Acting quickly, Simmons' appointed trustees secured mortgages for still prime center city acreage and rebuilt the Simmons rental properties. Only when those rental income funds returned to five-hundred thousand dollars, as John Simmons instructed in his will, were the trustees allowed to petition the Massachusetts legislature and incorporate the college—in 1899, more than twenty-five years after the Great Boston Fire. Trustees and women educators had all rallied to establish the college whose financial assets had been severely diminished. They rightly believed the college's mission was too important to abandon despite financial hardship. Finally, though delayed by fire, John Simmons' radical philanthropic dream was about to come true.

Unfortunately, because of the Great Boston Fire, Simmons College was never the tuition-free institution John may have intended. Nevertheless, Simmons' mission, as stated in Article 16 of his will, remained intact: "to found and endow an institution to be called 'Simmons Female College' for the purpose of teaching medicine, music, drawing, designing, telegraphy [telegraph technology] and other branches of art, science and industry best calculated to enable the scholars to acquire an independent livelihood." The college's purpose—a radical approach of combining a traditional college curriculum with career education—was unique in all of New England compared to other women's colleges, which emphasized a purely classical education.

Dorothea Dix so approved of this long awaited opportunity for women that she stipulated in her will that funds be set aside for women's education. Her executor, Horatio Appleton Lamb, was the treasurer at Simmons, and he facilitated the transfer of Dix's funds to Simmons College to subsidize "Dix Scholars" following her death in 1887.

300 The Fenway

When the time came to situate the college, the trustees followed the lead of their real estate investing founder: location, location, location. Prime land at 300 The Fenway was chosen and purchased from the Thayer Estate and the Water Department. Located directly across the street from Frederick Law Olmstead's Emerald Necklace, the eleven-thousand acre, seven-mile chain of greenery connecting nine Boston Parks from the Boston Common through Franklin Park in Roxbury, 300 The Fenway had access to superb public open areas.

It's of great interest and proof that Simmons' idea had many important female proponents, including Charlotte Burns Brooks, the wife of John Simmons' lawyer, Benjamin F. Brooks. She led the task force soliciting ideas for the nascent college. Her correspondence is preserved at the Schlesinger Library in Cambridge. Additionally, Catharine Beecher had been consulting with Simmons trustees before her death, and they clearly took her counsel about building a college in an urban setting. They selected the Fenway location instead of a Jamaicaway site, because it was closer to the city for budget-minded commuting students. The trustees especially wanted the college to be accessible to women from Roxbury and the South End, the very communities from whose labor pool of seamstresses John Simmons had made his fortune, and the Fenway area was ideal.

Providentially, Isabella Stewart Gardner had built her own Fenway Court near the rustic and rural area designed for recreation and contemplation. The widow of Jack Gardner, art collector Mrs. Gardner collaborated with architect Willard T. Sears. By then he had designed the Old South Church, and he was renowned for his work in the Gothic Revival and Renaissance Revival styles. Together, Sears and Mrs. Gardner designed a Venetian-style Renaissance palace where she lived until her death in 1924. In a mansion that included the first covered courtyard in America, Mrs. Gardner eclectically organized her legendary collection of Old Master and modern paintings. Works by Titian, Rembrandt, and Whistler each had pride of place. This patron of the arts lived on the fourth floor above her three-story art collection, now known as the Isabella Stewart Gardner Museum. In keeping with the manners of the times, Simmons trustees sought Mrs. Gardner's opinion regarding the location of Simmons College, and she did not object to the institution as her neighbor.

The Fenway area's residents increased and institutions grew when in 1906, Harvard Medical School moved from Copley Square to Longwood Avenue, directly behind Simmons College's Main Campus, which had been built in 1904. In 1909, the Museum of Fine Arts, Boston, completed the neighborhood with a temple-like structure designed by architect Guy Lowell, the landscape designer of the Boston Esplanade and a member of the Simmons College Corporation.

Simmons College

Simmons College's first building was designed by the prestigious firm of Peabody and Stearns in 1904. Architect Robert Swain Peabody (1845-1917) was the son of a Unitarian minister at King's Chapel in Boston. Peabody also designed the Breakers in Newport and Boston's Custom House Tower, which rose to four-hundred and ninety-six feet and was the tallest building in town when it was built in 1905. The Simmons Main Campus Building was so well constructed that it has served the community for over a century. Constructed in the Progressive Era, it is a highly functional space, matching the practical mission of the college.

The character of the school was formed during a twenty-nine-year waiting period, as the fire-ravaged land of Simmons' former investment properties was mortgaged, buildings rebuilt, and rent redeemed. Resiliency, patience and flexibility were key—and while the Great Boston Fire took much, it also brought to the fore the work ethic and self-reliance principles endorsed by John.

Because the college was never heavily endowed, students appreciated their education because of the personal financial sacrifices they made to attend. Productive, practical, highly motivated women echoed the qualities of their school's founder. Henry LeFavour, the first President of Simmons College, said in his opening remarks on October 9, 1902 that the new college should "lead the way with standards of the future rather than of the past." From its inception, Simmons classes prepared women for the labor force and for self-discovery.

Fannie Farmer

Fannie Farmer, of the Boston Cooking School fame, was at the end of her career when the college came into being. She sold equipment from her school to the Home Economics Department of Simmons College. Like John Simmons, Miss Farmer had her eye on her clientele. Just as John's customers had social ambitions, so did Miss Farmer's. She knew women that understood socially upscale cooking, including elaborate dinners, was key to upward mobility—

and many more women now had the leisure time to tend to the practice of cooking and fine dining. Like John in the clothing business, Miss Farmer recognized precise measurements were a key ingredient to successful meals.

Miss Farmer was an early proponent of standard tin measuring cups, a new product in her day. Until then, a cup was not a precise instrument; it depended on the size the owner had on hand. Like Simmons with his standard clothes sizes, Miss Farmer advocated accurate measurements. She held demonstration cooking classes twice weekly for one- to two-hundred students. Earlier in her life, as a seventeen-year-old high school student in Medford, Massachusetts, Miss Farmer contracted polio, and she spent the last seven years of her life in a wheelchair, yet she continued her work. This self-made, self-sufficient chef and cookbook author was the first woman to lecture at Harvard Medical School about diet and health. Because of her hard work and financial success, she purchased and lived in her own two-hundred thousand dollar nine-bedroom estate in Harvard, Massachusetts. Miss Farmer proudly named it Weldon, a mischievous play on the phrase "well-done." Like John Simmons, Miss Farmer died of Bright's Disease and she, too, is buried in Mount Auburn Cemetery in Cambridge.

Miss Farmer's contributions to the world of cooking and to Simmons College proved of lasting value, and today it's commonly accepted that the pleasures of fine meal preparation know no gender and that good food is the way to the romantic heart. Indeed, the

Simmons College home economics course that was based on Fannie's teachings was humorously dubbed "The Diamond Ring Class."

Early College Women

Who were the women who attended college at the turn of the twentieth century? Being in the vanguard, they were expected to be brave, independent intellectual females willing to ignore conservative critics who feared and even predicted educated women would abandon their domestic roles. Naysayers claimed early twentieth-century college women had limited energy and might hurt their "female apparatus" with too much mental work outside the home. College women had to overcome negative stereotypes—"Old maid," "infertile," "unruly," "unmarriageable"—all were epithets some early college women endured. In an effort to exclude women from academia, men often adamantly opposed the admission of women to their colleges. As a result, Radcliffe, Pembroke, Barnard, and Jackson College were established, a response which served to strengthen the effort to educate women. But in general, college women of the early twentieth century were not elite; only 7.3 percent of early female college grads came from the highest income families. In the early 1900s, upper class women were educated privately and studied in Europe. Colleges like Radcliffe were for upper middle-class women, daughters of professional class fathers with salaries three times the salaries of average workers—who had visions of upward mobility for their female offspring. As the women's educational movement took hold, women flocked to the doors of colleges, and

153

founders and donors continued their educational objectives. Smith College was founded by a woman, Sophia Smith, and Wellesley College was founded by a couple, Henry and Pauline Durant.

An Independent Livelihood

Simmons College originated as a woman's college because of one man's philanthropy and keen sense of the plight of women in his times. Historian Laurie Crumpacker describes the women who went to Simmons as unique even among their fellow female college attendees. "Simmons College," she writes "...made efforts at cross-class outreach by keeping its tuition lower than at elite schools, offering scholarships to those in need, and welcoming Jewish and African-American students when discrimination was still common at most other colleges. But most important...Simmons was committed to educating women who needed to work for a living." In 1910, Lydia Grinnell from New Bedford, Massachusetts was the first black student admitted to the college. She worked for the War Department in Washington, D.C. in 1914. After graduating with the Class of 1915, Lydia attended the Harvard Graduate School of Education.

Simmons students were like their college's founder in seeking opportunities to rise through the world of work. Following Simmons' example, college administrators strategically watched the marketplace and focused on professional areas of domestic science such as household economics. With the help of the faculty, administrators established first class schools of retailing, nursing, general science, social work and library science. Simmons College graduates have become instrumental leaders in these areas. The college's educational benefits included fostering an identity outside of one's family of origin and increasing self-confidence derived from successfully completing meaningful work. Simmons College provided the opportunity President Theodore Roosevelt treasured when he said, "Far and away the best prize that life has to offer is the chance to work hard at work worth doing."

Simmons College taught and continues to teach women skills for emerging professions. Graduates have always been praised as market responsive, because of the college's unwavering emphasis on preparing for work. John Simmons' bequest placed his faith in women of future generations. In 1870, he was survived by two daughters and two granddaughters. But today, this visionary businessman with a mission of social responsibility has more than sixty-thousand daughters, degree recipients from the beloved women's college that bears this generous tailor's name.

The Grave of John Simmons

Even in death, John Simmons carefully considered and provided for his extended family. Fifteen relatives are buried with John in his beautiful graveside Lot 585 on Central Avenue at Mt. Auburn Cemetery in Cambridge.

Photo courtesy of Denise Doherty Pappas.

AFTERWORD

It is wonderful to imagine John Simmons the man, in his time; to consider his life and the factors that motivated him and ultimately inspired his vision. If he were to be transported into the future, to present day 2014, well over a century after he drafted his will, what would he think of his College? Now a small university with five distinct graduate schools and his undergraduate women's college at the center, it is a place transformed.

He would certainly be surprised by the hustle and bustle of our campus—the modern dress and manner of the community and the expanded campus and twenty-first century architecture. He might be startled yet pleased to see his College nestled among a vast network of hospitals, social and cultural venues, and multitude of area colleges and universities.

Spending a day or two on campus, he would be delighted to observe his original ideals and mission alive and well—evident in the daily lives and experiences of Simmons students today. Our students, beneficiaries of his once radical vision, are now visionaries themselves, with their feet firmly planted—driven, focused, self-directed, and resourceful—they envision and realize bright futures for themselves, and take nothing for granted. Within our community, John Simmons would observe a strong tradition of peer mentoring among our students—and the powerful backdrop of many female role models in the administration and faculty who serve not only to inspire, but to mentor and motivate.

In an era where the value of a women's college education is increasingly scrutinized, and often perceived as no longer relevant, every day I observe the ways in which John Simmons' vision deeply benefits our students and how his College prepares them uniquely for meaningful lives and careers. As Dean of Students, I treasure my role and the opportunity to see young women be transformed before my eyes. In many respects, all of us at Simmons have a role in preserving his timeless vision, and through these core values we honor his vision in our daily encounters and work with our students.

His founding ethos of preparing women to earn an independent livelihood has evolved into producing graduates who serve as change agents in their chosen field of work, helping to pave the way for the next generation of women—continually paying it forward.

This was perfectly illustrated in a conversation with a recent graduate, now employed by the Massachusetts State House as a legislative aid for a state representative. She reflected on how the Simmons experience prepared her to navigate the complex political landscape of her job in an environment where women are still largely underrepresented in political office. Through a legislative internship funded by a generous Simmons alumna, she gained the experience critical to her employment. Today, she is setting the stage for her own political career: the path to a dream and a dream realized with more dreams yet to come.

In another recent conversation, a student poised to graduate reflected openly on her Simmons experience. As a first-generation college student, and the only daughter of immigrant parents, she silently struggled in her transition to college. A private education, even with scholarships and grants, was enormously expensive for her family. She wondered whether she truly belonged at Simmons. What if she couldn't cut it academically? She didn't want to let anyone down—she wanted to make her family proud, especially her father. But Simmons helped her develop what she called a "new attitude", which I read to mean courage: courage to stretch and to trust in herself and her potential. She was met by a faculty who both challenged her and encouraged her to challenge herself. She pursued internship and research opportunities and attended academic conferences that opened doors for her. With encouragement from her older classmates, she sought student leadership roles that developed her skill set, earning the respect of her peers and further bolstering her confidence. Raised in a culture which traditionally does not value education and careers for women, this was a dream that once seemed far out of reach, unattainable. Next fall she will attend dental school, fulfilling her dream of becoming a dentist. And so today, it is a dream realized.

How do these dreams materialize? Each year I have the honor of hosting an event where we celebrate the power of philanthropy at a Scholarship Appreciation Brunch. This event brings together our scholarship donors and student recipients and it's always a full house, with many students and alumnae in attendance. It is a powerful occasion where the donors come to understand first-hand the impact of their scholarship gifts, and students meet their scholarship donors face-to-face. There isn't a dry eye in the house. Student speakers opine on the transformative nature of their scholarships, absolute game changers in their lives They understand intuitively that with such opportunity comes responsibility to go out into the world, to pursue their passions and to do good. And to always give back. And so the cycle continues, lives are transformed and dreams materialize.

Today, we never question whether Simmons graduates will gain economic independence. We ask what mark they will make in their communities and in the world. What legacy will they leave behind at their beloved alma mater?

Thank you, Mr. Simmons. Legions of your graduates are giving back and changing the world in every discipline and in all walks of life. We at Simmons are deeply humbled by the works of your alumni, your like-minded sons and daughters. Politicians, teachers, librarians, nurses, social workers, business leaders, entrepreneurs and more, each graduating class ensures that deeds match words. Mr. Simmons, your grand vision endures.

Sarah Neill
Dean of Students
Simmons College
October 2014

ACKNOWLEDGMENTS

Who knew it would take a community to build a biography?

I am grateful to all who helped me bring John Simmons to the attention of a twenty-first century audience.

I would like to thank the Simmons Community, all those who know first hand the value of a Simmons education: Helen Drinan, President of Simmons College; Cheryl Howard, Vice President for Marketing and Admission; Sarah Neill, Vice President of Student Affairs and Dean of Students; Kathleen Rogers, Vice President and General Counsel; Jason Wood, College Archivist and Head of Discovery Services; Justin Snow, Library Assistant; Laura Prieto, Chair, Department of History; Cathryn Mercier, Director for the Study of Children's Literature; Laurie Crumpacker, Senior Lecturer, College of Arts and Sciences; Diane Hammer, Director, Simmons Institute for Leadership and Change; Len Mailloux, Senior Lecturer, Communications Department; Marianne Lord, Vice President of Advancement; Janice Taylor, Event Strategist; Dianne Cullinane, Assistant to the Vice President of Advancement; Linda Gallinaro, Associate Director of Strategic Events; Donna Dolan, Assistant Vice President, Academic Operations and Registrar; Courtney Dee, Director of Online Communications and Design; Mike Correia, Web Designer and Content Management Administrator; Reverend Bonnie-Jeanne Casey, Spiritual Life Program Manager; and Haley Lamson, Catherine Seely, and Claudia Haydon. Thanks to Steve and Carolyn

McCandless, and Janet Tobin for their encouragement of this biography. My sincerest thanks and admiration go to the talented and dedicated faculty of Simmons College who cultivate and inspire life-long learners. I am grateful to my fellow trustees and corporators for their leadership and generosity on behalf on Simmons College.

I am also most grateful for my experiences at the Norman Mailer Writing Center in Provincetown, Massachusetts, where this biography began—and where Ann Small Simmons was born. Special thanks go to Lawrence Schiller, President and Co-Founder of The Norman Mailer Center; and to J. Michael Lennon, Norman Mailer's archivist, editor and authorized biographer; and to Donna Pedro Lennon and Nina Wiener. I am forever thankful to Deborah Martinson, Professor and Chair, Writing and Rhetoric Department, Occidental College, whose invaluable advice and encouragement made this book possible, and to biographers Kylie Bolton, Judith Stein and Jacqueline Miller Byrd. Thanks, too, to Laurel Guadazno for her assistance at the Provincetown Monument and Museum.

Special gratitude to the *Provincetown Arts* staff whose high standards were matched by their generous critiques: Christopher Busa, Founder and Publisher, *Provincetown Arts*; Ingrid Aue, Marketing Director; and Susanna Ralli, Senior Editor.

All biographers rely on historical societies and libraries. This book is indebted to Little Compton Historical Society, located in the town where John Simmons was born, and where historians preserve and protect materials regarding John Simmons' life and legacy. Thanks to Marjory Gomez O'Toole, Managing Director of LCHS, and Piper Hawes, Little Compton Historical Society board member who enthusiastically guided me through the Society's collection and squired me through Little Compton. Thank you to Fred Bridge, Board Member, and summer resident Kris Montgomery.

My research was aided by librarians throughout the Commonwealth. Julie Kinchla, Head of Information Services at the Winchester, MA Public Library provided resources to me with unceasing patience and skill. At The Boston Athenaeum my thanks go to: Mary Warnement Head of Reference; Stanley Ellis Cushing, Curator of Rare Books and Manuscripts; and Catharina Slautterback, Curator of Prints and Photographs. Clare Sheridan, consulting librarian at the American Textile History Museum in Lowell, MA was very helpful. Kristen Gresh, Estrelita and Yousuf Karsh Assistant Curator of Photographs at the Museum of Fine Arts, Boston, provided good direction about photograph permissions. Thanks, too, to Jann Sheehy, Chair of the Program Committee of the Friends of the Winchester Public Library, archivist Mary LaBombard, and Kelvin Chen, an extraordinary research assistant.

I spent many a day walking through Mount Auburn Cemetery where John Simmons and his family are buried, and I owe a great deal to Meg Winslow. As Curator of Historical Collection there Meg graciously shared John Simmons' file with me at the Mount Auburn archive. Jane Carroll, Vice President of Development, encouraged my search along with Sarah Furbush Taraskiewicz, and Carol Harper, a superb tour guide, Simmons alumna and fan of John's.

Writers and Historians whose own work inspired me include: Stephanie Schorow, Pamela Tanner Boll, Reverend Sarah Gibb Millspaugh, Betsy Bowles, Kendall Dudley, Thomas E. Convery, and Dr. Joseph Valeriani. I deeply appreciate Dr. H. Edward Clark's many letters of encouragement. I am very grateful to my steadfast writing group—Lani Peterson Arnzen, Sara Epstein, Jane Gossard, Leontine Hartzell, and Roberta Whitney. Friends who gave me their ears and unwavering support include: my Winchester book groups, as well as Maria and Gunther Winkler, Jennifer Clifford, Lynn Hart Taber, Marsha and Ted Lamson, Kai and Andrew Chen, Larry and Linda Abramson, Katy Wolf, Susan and Tony Morris, Mary Collins, Richard Bowker, David Brody, Shanoo Saran, Leslie and John Iannuzzo, Elissa Traher, Bernie Kelley-Leccese, and the Gingrande, O'Neil and Habib families. Sara and Robert Depczenski were constant cheerleaders whose generous gift of a painted plaster cast from a John Rogers nineteenth century bronze statue, *Why Don't You Speak For Yourself, John?,* amused me and inspired my writing.

The following people generously shared their time and creative guidance. Lora Brody, Elaine Lindy (MBA 1985), Karen Davis of The Orton Gallery in Hudson, NY, Deborah Weinstein, Anne Speyer and Ann Bechan each read early manuscript drafts and made helpful suggestions. Emily Taber edited that work with patience and care; Eileen Kenneally, Principal, Kenneally Creative of Arlington, MA tirelessly and cheerfully created the graphics within the manuscript. Suzanne Goodwin was immensely helpful with graphic layout. Video artist Sam Smiley was a major asset in documenting Simmons' life. With great generosity, Sam meticulously photographed archival materials held by Simmons College and Little Compton Historical Society. I am grateful to Nina Lapchyk for assisting me in creating artworks relating to John Simmons. Renowned visual artist Lora Brody graciously photographed the author.

Special thanks to David Gullette, founder of Fenway Press, for his editorial expertise and enthusiasm for this project.

Above all, it was my good fortune to meet Catherine Parnell through Lora Body. As my editor, Catherine shaped this biography with astute observations, patient diplomacy and top-notch publishing expertise.

I am very grateful to my parents, Tom and Dot Doherty, now deceased, who supported my education in every way.

Finally, I'd like to thank my husband Dean Pappas and our sons, Greg and Justin Pappas and my daughter-in-law, Amy Menkin. Without their patience, encouragement and computer assistance, this book would have been but a dream.

Denise Doherty Pappas
October 2014

The author at age four with her uncle, John J. O'Neil, future publisher of *The Food and Nutrition Press* and author of *Bombs Away
By Pathfinders of the Eighth Air Force.*

READER'S GUIDE

For more than 100 years, the mission of Simmons College has been to provide an education that combines "intellectual leadership with professional preparation." None of this would be possible without John Simmons, a man of humble origin, whose hard work and vision led to the establishment of Simmons. Every year on Founder's Day, the community honors John Simmons, and in so doing, also honors his history, including the time-honored principle of social responsibility, which John Simmons, in his frock coat and cravat, embodies.

Chapter One: First Fortune

In this chapter, we learn about John Simmons' ancestors.

- Do you have a story about your ancestors?
- Where did your family originally come from?
- Why did they (or you) come to this country?
- What do you know about your ancestors—their faith, education, occupations?

Chapter Two: Opportunity Knocks

This chapter provides background for John Simmons' career as he moved from Little Compton, Rhode Island to Boston, Massachusetts.

- What was your first job?
- What was the economy like when you first starting working?

- How has the class structure changed since John's day?

Chapter Three: Production Costs

The tailoring trade and attitudes about dress are discussed in this chapter.

- Describe how you dressed when you first began working.
- How has your attitude toward clothes changed over the years?
- Do clothes still "make the man?"

Chapter Four: Times and Treasures

As John Simmons' business grew, his position in the social pyramid changed. This chapter describes the cultural expectations that come with affluence.

- Discuss the changes you have noticed in consumption of goods and services from your youth to the present day.
- Describe the effect of these changes on personal happiness.

Chapter Five: Ducats and Daughters

This section reports on the options and restrictions on women in the mid-nineteenth century.

- What do you recall or have you learned about the Women's Movement of the 1970s and beyond?

- In what specific ways have women's lives improved? Can you cite specific ways in which you find progress lacking?

Chapter Six: Is it Fair?

Slavery and immigration were huge moral and social issues in John's time, and the memory of the injustice, cruelty, brutality, and inhumanity of people as chattel has been passed down through the generations. Immigration reform is a highly politicized topic that has also been a part of the history of the U.S.

- Although slavery is illegal in the U.S., where do you see as its effects today?
- What do you believe are the key issues about present day U.S. immigration?

Chapter Seven: Half of My Life is Gone

Literature and poetry can articulate ideas about the purpose of life and the passage of time. One of the best-known examples would be the writings of Benjamin Franklin, who wisely said: "The doors of wisdom are never shut."

- What movies, plays, biographies, fiction, non-fiction and poetry have helped you recognize and express "the meaning of life"?

Chapter Eight: Thy Will Be Done

John Simmons' endowment of a college is revealed in this chapter. Rather than leave his fortune to his family, John Simmons placed a metaphorical cornerstone in his city which ensured educational opportunities for generations of women (and men!).

- Are there any tangible objects you would like to leave behind?
- What are your feelings about leaving a legacy?
- How would you like to be remembered?

Chapter Nine: Wheel of Fortune

The Great Boston Fire of 1872 thwarts John's plan, but Simmons College rises nonetheless.

- What are your "setback" stories? What were the final results?
- Is adversity really the best teacher?

John Simmons' Wheel of Fortune

Lawyer's explanation "To make a return to that class of women by whose labor he had laid the foundation of his fortune."

Capitalist guilt

No male heirs

Admiration for his work staff

Possible Motivations for Endowment of Simmons College

Influence of wife and mother

Example of Matthew Vassar

Regard for unknown person

Desire for immortality

Experience with daughters

Unitarian belief in equality of men and women

SUPPLEMENT TO THE READER'S GUIDE

LOOKING BACK

1. Can you recall an image/photo—real or virtual—of yourself during your college years? What were you like then? What were your dreams, concerns, causes, loves and goals?

2. What is your story about choosing the college you attended? Are you glad you attended that college? Why or why not?

3. How would you describe your college experience academically? Socially? Emotionally? How did you change from your freshman to senior year?

4. Did you have a professor or college friend who remains memorable? What story can you tell to describe that person and his/her long lasting effect on you?

5. Have you ever attended a college class reunion? Why or why not?

6. Name three big changes in society since your college days.

GIVING BACK

1. John Simmons left behind his Bible, an oil portrait, and some of his china. Perhaps through these objects we can glean something of his values, taste and position in society. What three objects would you put into a time capsule to help someone in the future understand your life and times?

2. Do you keep a diary or journal or blog? Why or why not?

3. John Simmons' reputation comes from donating a large portion of his fortune to start a college for women so that they might gain "an independent livelihood." What would you like said about you by future generations?

4. In his will, John Simmons left his daughters funds so they would be comfortable, but not wealthy. What do you think of his decision?

5. What is your favorite philanthropic cause or charitable organization? How did you become involved with that mission?

6. Have you given back to your college? Why or why not?

LOOKING FORWARD

1. John Simmons' legacy helped women to push forward through college education, a radical idea in his day. What is your opinion of single sex education today? What do you feel are its advantages and disadvantages? What types of educational institutions and enterprises do you envision for the future?

2. What do you think a college education should provide?

3. Imagine our future. What innovations in the arts and sciences might advance society? For example, what is today's equivalent of the sewing machine?

4. Reformers always play a significant role in shaping society. Name two present-day leaders you expect will impact the future. How might this happen?

LIST OF ILLUSTRATIONS

BIBLIOGRAPHY

Alden Kindred of America, Inc. "The Aldens in American Culture." *Alden House Historic Site.* Accessed on August 1, 2013. http://www.alden.org/pilgrim_lore/courtship.html.

Ames, Samuel. *Reports of the Cases Argued and Determined in the Supreme Court of Rhode Island.* Vol. 1, *Rhode Island Reports.* Boston: Little, Brown and Company, 1858.

American Transcendentalism Web. "[Sarah] Margaret Fuller: 1810-1850." Accessed June 8, 2011. http://transcendentalism-legacy.tamu.edu/authors/fuller/index.html.

———. "Margaret Fuller: The Great Lawsuit. Man versus Men." Woman versus Women." Accessed June 8, 2011. http://transcendentalism-legacy.tamu.edu/authors/fuller/debate.html.

———. "Social Reform: Margaret Fuller and her *Conversations.*" Accessed June 8, 2011. http://transcendentalism-legacy.tamu.edu/authors/fuller/conversations-mf.html.

Amos Adams Lawrence Papers. "Guide to the Collection." Boston: Massachusetts Historical Society. Accessed July 17, 2014. http://www.masshist.org/collection-guides/view/fa0166.

Ancestry.com. *1850 United States Federal Census.* Provo, UT: Ancestry.com Operations, Inc., 2009.

———. *1870 United States Federal Census.* Provo, UT: Ancestry.com Operations, Inc., 2009.

———. *1900 United States Federal Census.* Provo, UT: Ancestry.com Operations Inc., 2004.

————. *Massachusetts, Death Records, 1841-1915.* Provo, UT: Ancestry.com Operations, Inc., 2013.

————. *Massachusetts, Town and Vital Records, 1620-1988.* Provo, UT: Ancestry.com Operations, Inc., 2011.

————. *The New England Historical & Genealogical Register, 1847-2011.* Provo, UT: Ancestry.com Operations, Inc., 2011.

————. *U.S. Passport Applications, 1795-1925.* Provo, UT: Ancestry.com Operations, Inc., 2007.

Barre Patriot. "Can't Be Beat!" May 29, 1846, 3.

Bales, Richard. *Did the Cow Do It?: A New Look at the Cause of the Great Chicago Fire.* "Testimony." Accessed July 17, 2014. http://www.thechicagofire.com/testimony.php.

Bassett, Lynne Z. *Textiles for Regency Clothing, 1800-1850: A Workbook of Swatches and Information.* Arlington, VA: Q Graphics Production Co., 2002.

Boston Athenaeum. "Mission and History." Accessed March 1, 2014. http://bostonathenaeum.org/node/38.

Boston Architecture. "1 Arlington Street." Accessed August 1, 2013. http://www.bosarchitecture.com/backbay/arlington/1.html.

————. "2 Arlington Street." Accessed August 1, 2013. http://www.bosarchitecture.com/backbay/arlington/2.html.

————. "3 Arlington Street." Accessed August 1, 2013. http://www.bosarchitecture.com/backbay/arlington/3.html.

————. "222 Beacon Street." Accessed February 28, 2014. http://www.bosarchitecture.com/backbay/beacon/222.html.

Boston Daily Advertiser. "The Will of John Simmons." September 10, 1870, 1.

Boston Daily Atlas. "When We See an Establishment Like George W. Simmons' Oak Hall." September 27, 1849, 2.

Boston Directory for the Year 1852 Embracing the City Record, A General Directory of the Citizens, and a Business Directory, with an Almanac, From July 1852 to July 1853. Boston: Published by George Adams, 1852.

Boston University. "Our Place in History." July 17, 2014. http://www.bu.edu/admissions/about-bu/history.

Brattle Street Church. Accessed May 22, 2011. http://en.wikipedia.org/wiki/Brattle_Street_Church.

Bright's Disease. Accessed March 1, 2014. http://en.wikipedia.org/wiki/Bright%27s_Disease.

Brooks Brothers. Accessed May 23, 2011. http://www.brooksbrothers.com/about-us /about-us,default,pg.html.

Brown, Thomas T. *Dorothea Dix: New England Reformer.* Cambridge, MA: Harvard University Press, 1998.

Brownell, Carlton C. "John Simmons, Merchant Tailor." Simmons Family Collection. Little Compton, RI: Little Compton Historical Society, 1999.

Bunting, Bainbridge. *Houses of Back Bay: An Architectural History 1840-1917.* Cambridge, MA: Belknap Press, 1967.

Calhoun, Charles C. *Longfellow: A Rediscovered Life.* Boston: Beacon Press, 2004.

Canellos, Peter S. "Crowding, Conflict, and Conflagration." *Boston Globe.* March 2, 1997, 22.

Carey, Mark. "Inventing Caribbean Climates: How Science, Medicine, and Tourism Changed Tropical Weather from Deadly to Healthy." *Osiris* 26, no. 1 (2011): 129-141.

Carr, Vickie. "Paul Revere's Canton Years." Canton, MA: Canton Historical Society. Accessed June 18, 2012. http://www.canton.org/history/revere1.htm.

Chambers, Jacqueline. "Thinking and Stitching." In *Famine and Fashion: Needlewomen in the Nineteenth Century,* edited by Beth Harris. Burlington, Vermont: Ashgate Publishing, 2005.

Channing, William Ellery. *Memoir of William Ellery Channing, Vol II.* London: George Routledge and Company, Soho Square, 1850. Google Books.

Charlotte F. Brooks Papers. Schlesinger Library, Radcliffe College. Cambridge, MA.

Cheski, Susan. "John Simmons." *The Simmons News* 64, no. 7 (1986).

Chicago Historical Society. "The Chicago Fire." *The History Files.* Last modified 1999. http:www.chicagohs.org/history/fire.html.

Church, Lucy M. "Old Days in Little Compton." *The Simmons Quarterly* 2, no. 1 (1911):1-6.

Clark, Christopher. *Social Change in America: From the Revolution Through the Civil War.* Chicago: Ivan R. Dee, 2006.

Clark, Thomas, "A Legal Meeting of the Freeholders and Other Inhabitants of the Town of Boston." Boston: True and Greene, 1822.

Cobrin, Harry A. *The Men's Clothing Industry: Colonial Through Modern Times.* New York: Fairchild Publications, Inc., 1970.

Cowan, Ruth Schwartz. *More Work for Mother.* New York: Basic Book Publishers, 1983.

Crumpacker, Laurie. "Beyond Servants and Salesgirls: Working Women's Education in Boston, 1885-1915." In *Women of the Commonwealth: Work, Family, and Social Change in Nineteenth Century Massachusetts,* edited by Susan L. Porter. Amherst, MA: University of Massachusetts Press, 1996.

Dalzell, Robert F., Jr. *Enterprising Elite: The Boston Associates and the World They Made.* Cambridge, MA: Harvard University Press, 1987.

Davis, Lance Edwin, and Peter Lester Payne. "From Benevolence to Business: The Story of Two Savings Banks." *The Business History Review,* Vol. 32, No.4 (Winter, 1958) pg. 386-406, The President and Fellows of Harvard College. Accessed October 6, 2013. http:// www.jstor.org/stable/3111660.

Diner, Hasia. *Erin's Daughters in America: Irish Immigrant Women in the 19th Century.* Baltimore: John Hopkins University Press, 1983.

Dodd, Jordan, Liahona Research, comp. *Massachusetts, Marriages, 1633-1850.* Provo, UT: Ancestry.com Operations Inc., 2005.

Edirisooriya, Gunapala. "A market analysis of the latter half of the nineteenth century American higher education sector." *History of Education,* Vol. 38, No.1, January 2009.

Evans, Harold, Gail Buckland, and David Lefer. *They Made America: From the Steam Engine to the Search Engine: Two Centuries of Innovators.* Boston: Little, Brown and Company, 2004.

Feldman, Enid, and Penelope Kavageorge. "John Simmons' Rhode Island House." *Simmons Review* 39, no. 4 (Summer 1957).

Friends of Mt. Auburn. "Mount Auburn Consecrated."
Last modified December 8, 2011.
http://mountauburn.org/2011/consecration/.

Fuller, Margaret. "Woman in the Nineteenth Century: Part 1."
Accessed June 8, 2011. http://transcendentalism-
legacy.tamu.edu/authors/fuller/woman1.html.

Gabler-Hover, Janet, and Robert Sattelmeyer, eds. "The Autocrat of
the Breakfast-Table." *American History Through Literature.*
Volume 1. Gale Cengage, 2006. Accessed August 1, 2013.
http://www.enotes.com/autocrat-breakfast-table-reference/.

Gates, Henry Louis, Jr. *Life Upon These Shores: Looking at African
American History, 1513-2008.* New York: Knopf, 2011.

Golding, Claire. Untitled Article. *The Simmons Review* 56, no. 4: 2.

Goodwin, Claire. Notes on Little Compton. Boston, MA: Simmons
College Archives. May 1, 1999.

Goodwin, Joan. "Margaret Fuller." *Dictionary of Unitarian and
Universalist Biography.* Accessed August 1, 2013.
http://www.uua.org/uuhs/duub/articles/margaretfuller.html.

Graham, Patricia Albjerg. "Expansion and Exclusion: A History of
Women in American Higher Education." *Signs* 3, no. 4
(1978): 759-773.

Harris, Beth. "All That Glitters." In *Famine and Fashion: Needlewomen in the Nineteenth Century,* edited by Beth Harris.
Burlington, Vermont: Ashgate Publishing, 2005.

Hartford, William F. *Money, Morals, and Politics: Massachusetts in
the Age of the Boston Associates.* Boston: Northeastern University Press, 2001.

Hawes, Piper. "John Simmons, 1796-1870: Founder of Simmons College." *Portraits in Time*. Little Compton, RI: Little Compton Historical Society, 2008.

"History of Men's Wear Industry, 1890-1950." *Men's Wear* 121, no. 1 (1950), 193-344. New York: Fairchild Publications.

History Project. *Improper Bostonians: Lesbian and Gay History from the Puritans to Playland*. Boston: Beacon Press, 1998.

Holmes, Oliver Wendell. *The Autocrat of the Breakfast-Table*. Boston: Phillips, Sampson and Company, 1845. Google Books.

Homans, Isaac Smith, ed. *Hunt's Merchants' Magazine and Commercial Review*, 1845. Google Books.

Hood, Thomas. "Song of the Shirt. Accessed July 14, 2014. http://www.poets.org/poetsorg/poem/song-shirt.

Horowitz, Helen Lefkowitz. *Alma Mater: Design and Experience in the Women's College from Their Nineteenth Century Beginnings to the 1930's*. New York: Knopf, 1984.

Horton, James Oliver, and Lois E. Horton. *Black Bostonians: Family Life and Community Struggle in the Antebellum North*. New York: Holmes and Meier, 1999.

Howe, Daniel Walker. *Making the American Self: Jonathan Edwards to Abraham Lincoln*. Oxford: Oxford University Press, 2009.

———. *What Hath God Wrought: The Transformation of America, 1815-1848*. Oxford: Oxford University Press, 2009.

Howells, William Dean. *The Rise of Silas Lapham*. New York: Dodd, Mead, and Co., 1964.

Hunt, Freeman, ed. *The Merchant's Magazine and Commercial Review* 1848. Google Books.

"John Simmons Never Searched for His Roots...He Planted Them." *The Simmons Review* 60, no. 1 (1977).

The Juilliard School. "A Brief History." *About Juilliard.* Accessed on August 1, 2013. http://www.juilliard.edu/about/history.php.

The Junior League of Boston Presents the Twenty-First Annual Decorators' Show House and Garden Tour. Boston: The League, 1991.

Kalman, Maria. *The Principles of Uncertainty.* New York: Penguin Group, 2007.

Karr, Arnold J. *Two Centuries of American Men's Wear.* Washington, DC: Apparel Retailers of American, 1993.

Kelly, Martin. "Seneca Falls Convention: Background and Details." *About.com: American History.* Last modified 2013. http://www.americanhistory.about.com/od/womenssuffrage/a/senecafalls.htm.

Kidwell, Claudia B., and Margaret C. Christman. *Suiting Everyone: The Democratization of Clothing in America.* Washington, D.C.: Smithsonian Institution Press, 1974.

Kimball, Christopher. *Fannie's Last Supper: Re-creating One Amazing Meal from Fannie Farmer's 1896 Cookbook.* New York: Hyperion, 2010.

Knapp, Mary L. *An Old Merchant's House: Life at Home in New York City, 1835-65.* New York: Girandole Books and Merchant's House Museum, 2012.

Larkin, Jack. *The Reshaping of Everyday Life, 1790-1840.* New York: Harper and Row, 1988.

Lasser, Carol, and Stacey Robertson. *Antebellum Women: Private, Public, Partisan.* Lanham, Maryland: Rowman and Littlefield Publishers, Inc., 2010.

Lee, Hermione. *Biography: A Very Short Introduction.* Oxford: Oxford University Press, 2009.

LeFavour, Henry. "The Will of John Simmons." *The Simmons Quarterly* 1, no. 3 (1911): 1-9.

Lincoln, Levi. "Boston Courier Report of The Union Meeting in Faneuil Hall, Thursday, Dec.8, 1859." Boston: Clark, Fellows and Company, 1859. Accessed February 23, 2014. Google Books.

Lothrup, Thornton Kirkland, ed. "My Ministry at the Church in Brattle Square, Boston." *Some Reminiscences of the Life of Samuel Kirkland Lothrop.* Cambridge, MA: John Wilson and Son, 1888. Google Books.

"Lydia Booth." In *Vassar Encyclopedia.* Accessed March 23, 2009. http://vcencyclopedia.vassar.edu/index.php?title=LydiaBooth .html.

Mackintosh, Sheila. "Sarah Soule Wilbour, 1804-1891: Activist Author." *Portraits in Time.* Little Compton, RI: Little Compton Historical Society, 2008.

Macon Weekly Telegraph. "The Ten Richest Men or Estates in Boston." June 16, 1866, 4.

Malcolm, Janet. *Two Lives: Gertrude and Alice.* New Haven: Yale University Press, 2007.

Mamunes, George. *"So Has a Daisy Vanished": Emily Dickinson and Tuberculosis.* Jefferson, NC: McFarland and Company, 2008.

"Margaret Fuller." Accessed July 29, 2014.
http://en.wikipedia.org/wiki/Margaret_Fuller.

Mark, Kenneth L. *Delayed by Fire: Being the Early History of Simmons College.* Concord, NH: Rumford Press, 1945.

Marshall, Megan. *The Peabody Sisters.* Boston: Houghton Mifflin, 2005.

"Matthew Vassar." In *Vassar Encyclopedia.* Accessed January 14, 2012. http:// vcencyclopedia.vassar.edu/matthre-vassar/matthew-vassar.html.

McPherson, James M. *The Illustrated Battle Cry of Freedom: The Civil War Era.* Oxford: Oxford University Press, 2003.

McWilliams, John. *New England's Crises and Cultural Memory: Literature, Politics, History, Religion 1620-1860.* New York: Cambridge University Press, 2004. Google Books.

Merrill, Lisa. *When Romeo was a Woman: Charlotte Cushman and Her Circle of Female Spectators.* Ann Arbor: University of Michigan Press, 1999.

Moran, Karen Board. "William Lloyd Garrison." *Worcester Women's History Project.* Accessed July 25, 2014.
http://www.wwhp.org/Resources/Slavery/williamlloydgarrison.html.

Moriarty, Dana. "Elizabeth Peabody and Fuller's 'Conversations'." *Social and Political Reform.* Accessed June 8, 2011.
http://transcendentalism-legacy.tamu.edu/ideas/conversations-epp.html.

Morgenroth, Lynda. *Boston Firsts: 40 Feats of Innovation and Invention that Happened First in Boston and Helped Make America Great.* Boston: Beacon Press, 2006.

Muckenhoupt, Margaret. *Dorothea Dix: Advocate for Mental Health Care.* Oxford: Oxford University Press, 2003.

National Park Service. "Seneca Falls in 1848." *Women's Rights.* Last modified July 29, 2013. http://nps.gov/wori/historyculture/seneca-falls-in-1848.htm.

National Portrait Gallery. *The Seneca Falls Convention: July 19-20, 1848.* Accessed August 1, 2013. http://www.npg.si.edu/col/seneca/senfalls1.htm.

Nelles, Walter. "Commonwealth v. Hunt." *Columbia Law Review* 32, no. 7 (1932): 1128-1169.

Newport Mercury. "State of Rhode Island and Providence Plantations." July 26, 1856, 4.

Nichols, Pamela. "Scarlett's Sisters." In *Famine and Fashion: Needlewomen in the Nineteenth Century,* edited by Beth Harris. Burlington, Vermont: Ashgate Publishing, 2005.

Norris, William. "Abbott Lawrence in *The Confidence Man:* American Success or American Failure?" Accessed July 27, 2014. https://journals.ku.edu/index.php/amerstud/article/viewFile/2322/2281.

North, S. N. D., ed. *Bulletin of the National Association of Wool Manufacturers.* Boston: Rockwell and Churchill, 1901.

"Notes. Literary." *The Nation* 11, no. 273 (September 22, 1870): 190-191.

O'Connor, Thomas H. *Bibles, Brahmins, and Bosses: A Short History of Boston.* Boston: Trustees of the Public Library of the City of Boston, 1976.

———. *Boston: A to Z.* Cambridge: Harvard University Press, 2000.

————. *The Hub: Boston Past and Present*. Boston: Northeastern University Press, 2001.

————. *Lords of the Loom: The Cotton Whigs and the Coming of the Civil War*. New York: Scribner and Sons, 1968.

Papers Relating to the Introduction of Pure Water. Boston: John H. Eastburn City Printer, 1838.

Patten, David. "S'cunnet Native had 13,000 Daughters." *Providence Journal*. February 14, 1955, 16.

Perez, Louis A., Jr., ed. *Slaves, Sugar, and Colonial Society: Travel Accounts of Cuba, 1801-1899*. Wilmington: Scholarly Resources, 1992.

"Private and Special Statuets of the General Court, Commonwealth of Massachusetts from June 1814 to Feb. 1822." Vol. V, Boston: Wells and Lilly, 1823.

Puleo, Stephen. *A City So Grand: The Rise of an American Metropolis*. Boston: Beacon Press, 2010.

Redniss, Lauren. *Radioactive: A Tale of Love and Fallout*. New York: It Books/Harper Collins, 2010.

Reed, Roger C. "History of One Arlington Street." *Show House Magazine*. February 1997, 14-15, 1997.

Reuben, Paul P. "Chapter 4: American Transcendentalism: A Brief Introduction." *PAL: Perspectives in American Literature, A Research and Reference Guide*. Last modified October 24, 2011. http://www.csustan.edu/english/reuben/pal/chap4/4intro.html

Richardson, Peter Tufts. *The Boston Religion: Unitarianism in Its Capital City*. Rockland, Maine: Red Barn Publishing, 2003.

Ritchie, Susan. "The Peabody Sisters." *Dictionary of Unitarian and Universalist Biography.* Accessed August 1, 2013. http://www.uua.org/uuhs/duub/articles/peabodysisters.html.

Rivard, Paul. *A New Order of Things: How the Textile Industry Transformed New England.* Hanover, NH: University Press of New England, 2002.

Rosenberg, Chaim M. *The Great Workshop: Boston's Victorian Age.* Charleston, SC: Arcadia Publishing, 2004.

———. *The Life and Times of Francis Cabot Lowell, 1775-1817.* Lexington, MA: Lexington Books, 2011.

Rowe, Henry S. *The Ancestry of John Simmons: Founder of Simmons College.* Cambridge, MA: The Riverside Press, 1933.

Salem Register. "A Neat Uniform." April 29, 1850, p 2.

Sammarco, Anthony Mitchell. *The Great Boston Fire of 1872: Images of America Series.* Dover, NH: Arcadia Publishing, 1997.

Schorman, Rob. *Selling Style: Clothing and Social Change at the Turn of the Century.* Philadelphia: University of Pennsylvania Press, 2003.

Schorow, Stephanie. *Boston on Fire: A History of Fires and Fire-fighting in Boston.* Beverly, MA: Commonwealth Editions, 2003.

Schwartz, Harold. "Fugitive Slave Days in Boston." *The New England Quarterly* 27, no. 2 (1954): 191-212.

———. *Samuel Gridley Howe: Social Reformer, 1801-1876.* Cambridge, MA: Harvard University Press, 1956.

Scott, Anne Firor. "The Ever Widening Circle: The Diffusion of Feminist Values from the Troy Female Seminary, 1822-1872." *History of Education Quarterly* 19, no. 1 (1979): 3-25.

"The Simmons Female College." *The College Courant* 7, no. 10 (September 17, 1870): 160-161.

Simmons, Lorenzo Albert. *History of the Simmons Family from Moses Simmons, 1st.* Lincoln, Nebraska: 1930.

"The Simmons Story." *The Simmons Review* 35, no. 1 (1952).

Sklar, Kathryn Kish. *Catharine Beecher: A Study in American Domesticity.* New York: Norton and Company, 1976.

Sniffin-Marinoff, Megan, and Peggy Loeb. "The Houses that John Simmons Built: A Self Guided Tour." *The Simmons Review* (1990).

Solomon, Barbara Miller. *In the Company of Educated Women.* New Haven: Yale University Press, 1985.

Sprague, William D. "Thomas Baldwin, D.D.1782-1826." *Annals of the American Pulpit.* New York: Robert Carter and Brothers, 1860. Accessed June 15, 2013. Google Books.

Stern, Judith E. "The Genesis of the Philadelphia School of Design for Women." University of Pennsylvania, 1975.

The Stranger's Guide in the City of Boston; Containing a Safe and Clear Directory of Some of the Most Reputable Business Houses in the City: a Valuable Book of Reference for Strangers and Residents. Boston: Andrews and Company, 1848.

Tate, Sheila. "Fortune." *Immigrant Ships Transcribers Guild.* Last modified August 14, 1999. http://www.immigrantships.net/v2/1600v2/fortune16211109.html.

"Thursday, Messr. John Simmons." *The Liberator.* May 9, 1851, 19. Boston.

"Tuberculosis." Accessed March 1, 2014. http://en.wikipedia.org/wiki/Tuberculosis.

Viney, Wayne. "Dorothea Dix." *Dictionary of Unitarian and Universalist Biography.* Accessed August 1, 2013. http://www.uua.org/uuhs/duub/articles/dorotheadix.html.

Wass, Ann Buermann, and Michelle Webb Fandrich. *Clothing Through American History: The Federal Era Through Antebellum, 1780-1860.* Santa Barbara, CA: Greenwood Publishing Group, 2010.

Wilbour, Sarah Soule. "Notes on some Compton men who have made their mark in other places." Newport, RI: Newport Historical Society, Box 29-4.

Wilson, Everett Broomall. *Early America at Work: A Pictorial Guide to Our Vanishing Occupations.* New York: A.S. Barnes, 1963.

Wilson, Mark R. *The Business of Civil War: Military Mobilization and the State, 1861-1865.* Baltimore: John Hopkins University Press, 2006.

Wren, Daniel A. "American Business Philanthropy and Higher Education in the Nineteenth Century." *The Business History Review* 57, no. 3 (1983): 321-346.

Wright, Conrad Edick. *American Unitarianism, 1805-1865.* Boston: Massachusetts Historical Society: Northeastern University Press, 1989.

Wright, Conrad Edick, and Katheryn P. Viens. *Entrepreneurs: The Boston Business Community, 1700-1850.* Boston: Massachusetts Historical Society, 1997.

Zakim, Michael. *Ready-Made Democracy: A History of Men's Dress in the American Republic, 1760-1860.* Chicago: University of Chicago Press, 2003.

ABOUT THE AUTHOR

Photo courtesy of Lora Brody.

Presently a trustee at Simmons College in Boston, Denise Doherty Pappas is a lifelong world traveler. Her joy has been teaching English and working with various writing groups: third graders, blue-collar teens, college students, Middle Eastern diplomats, international housewives and significance-seeking older adults. This is her first book. For more information, visit www.JohnSimmonsBiography.com.

Made in the USA
Charleston, SC
07 October 2014